BOXING IN SOUTH YORKSHIRE

Best Wishes

Ronnie Wharton

BOXING
IN SOUTH YORKSHIRE

by
Ronnie Wharton

Wharncliffe Books

Dedication

To the memory of all the late South Yorkshire Boxing Champions, especially Tommy Gummer, Henry Hall, Bruce Woodcock and also Jim Emmett, a boxing promoter in the 1930s and Jim Mahoney, a top referee throughout the 1930s and 1940s who were extremely helpful during the research for this book.

I would also like to thank Bill Matthews and Giles Brearley for supplying the majority of photographs used in this book and Ann-Marie Leach for putting the work on to disc.

First Published in 2000 by
Wharncliffe Books
an imprint of
Pen and Sword Books Limited,
47 Church Street, Barnsley,
South Yorkshire. S70 2AS

Copyright © Ronnie Wharton 2000

For up-to-date information on other titles produced under the Wharncliffe imprint, please telephone or write to:

> **Wharncliffe Books**
> **FREEPOST**
> **47 Church Street**
> **Barnsley**
> **South Yorkshire S70 2BR**
> **Telephone (24 hours): 01226 - 734555**

ISBN: 1-871647-85-1

A CIP catalogue record of this book is available from the British Library

Cover illustration: Johnny Cuthbert top left, Henry Hall top right, Prince Naseem Hamed in centre.

Printed in Great Britain by
Redwood Books, Trowbridge, Wiltshire

CONTENTS

ABOUT THE AUTHOR

Ronnie Wharton's first interest in boxing came from the early fifties radio boxing nights and the broadcasts of commentator Eamonn Andrews and his summariser, James Barrington-Dalby. A collector of scrap books and memorabilia since those early days led to him writing a successful series of newspaper articles on the history of the sport, published in the later seventies and very early eighties. Continued interest in a series he did for the *Sheffield Star* and the boxing explosion in South Yorkshire over the last twenty years, has led him to compile *Boxing in South Yorkshire*. Ronnie's first involvement with Wharncliffe came last year when he was one of the contributors to the highly successful *Aspects of Bradford*, a history of his hometown.

Boxing in South Yorkshire is the first book in a proposed series on boxers from Northern England, the next planned edition will be prominent boxers from the West Riding, particularly Leeds and Bradford.

Bibliography

A Century of Boxing Greats, Patrick Myler, Robson Books 1997.
The Paddy and the Prince, Nick Pitt, Yellow Jersey 1998.
Jack Solomons Tells All, Jack Solomons, Rich and Cowan, 1952.
Various Boxing Board of Control Year Books 1985 to the Present, edited by Barry J. Hugman

PART ONE
1890 TO THE SECOND WORLD WAR

GEORGE CORFIELD

The man who did most to popularise boxing in South Yorkshire during the pioneer days of glove fighting in the 1890s, was Sheffield's first boxing idol George Corfield. During his career George had the distinction of fighting for a world title, a feat that wasn't equalled by a boxer from the area until fifty years later, when Bruce Woodcock fought for a World crown. However, to save any arguments, it is fair to say, and meaning no disrespect to either fighter, that both contests went unrecognised worldwide.

George was born in New Cross in 1872, but by the time he was three months old, his parents had moved to Sheffield. His first appearance in the ring was made in a competition for all weights, organised by Frank Howson at the *Gaiety* music hall in July 1890. George's debut only lasted two rounds before he was knocked out by another Sheffielder, Harry Clarke. At another competition the following February at the Grand Music Hall, he came up against Clarke again. At this second meeting, Clarke was disqualified for knocking George off the stage, George going on to win the award. Later in the year he beat Bob Fleming at catchweight for

George Corfield, Sheffield's first boxing idol. (*Photo loaned by Bill Matthews*).

£20, Fleming being counted out in the sixth round. Fleming's brother 'Dot' fancied a go at George and the pair boxed a twenty-one round draw at the Norfolk Drill Hall.

In 1892 he fought the 10lb heavier Frank Kenny at Sangers Circus at catchweight and lost on a foul in the eighth round. This was followed by a fourth round win over Harry Lowe at the same venue.

George's progress as a fighter in the city was only rivalled by the man who had beaten him on his ring debut, and it was an obvious conclusion that there would have to be another meeting between the two. The result was Sheffield's first big money match under Marquis of Queensbury rules.

After articles had been signed for £100 a man and the gate money, it was the start of a great upsurge of interest in boxing in Sheffield, and to witness the encounter between the two rivals, it was estimated that there were between seven to ten thousand people in the Norfolk Drill Hall. Clarke was the older by six years; he had yet to be beaten and had won sixteen competitions. Clarke was taken in hand by former Sheffield fighter, and then promoter, Frank Howson, whilst George went to Leicester to complete his training under the guidance of the Wilson brothers, a noted boxing family. The fight went the full fifteen rounds. George had the advantage of weight, but Clarke was a great battler, and he tried all he knew to protect his unbeaten record.

In the two years since that first match, George had improved in leaps and bounds, and although the fight went the distance, it was obvious after ten rounds, there was only one winner.

After his win, George felt the adoration of the Sheffield crowd, and it was from this moment that he became their adopted hero. So much so that brass bands conducted him from his training quarters to the hall where he fought. He sold silk favours by the dozen to his admirers at a guinea a time, and it was a regular occurrence to see him carried shoulder high through the streets of Sheffield surrounded by cheering masses.

George's next opponent was W. Wilson of Leeds, again at the Norfolk Drill Hall in January 1893 in a match arranged at 7 stone 12lb and for £500-a-side plus gate money. Wilson had made his name in competitions in London and was expected to give the Sheffielder a good fight. Betting was five guineas to four pounds on Corfield. Wilson put up a game fight but was well beaten, the fight ending in the fourteenth round, when the bloodied Wilson, beaten to a standstill by the power of George's punches, was unable to continue.

Three months later George met Joe Morton at the Drill Hall for the same sidestakes as in his last fight. Morton, who hailed from Nottingham, boxed out of Alfreton. He was the protege of 'The Brick Lad' (the nickname of Sheffield pugilist W. Stanton). Stanton had been training Morton at his father's Public House, *The Traveller's Rest,* at Alfreton and there was a gathering from the village to witness the encounter.

George's clever in-fighting soon began to make its mark and it quickly became a question of how long Morton would last. For one moment it looked as if things might go sour but there was never any doubt about the winner. Morton was so well beaten that in the latter stages, George Wilson - Corfield's backer and second - thinking that Morton was, in fact, giving up, entered the ring to hail the winner. There was a strong appeal by Morton's corner that the second had interfered and Corfield should be disqualified. Fortunately, the referee overruled the claim, so George duly stepped back into the ring. The completion of his execution put the result beyond any doubt, the knockout occurring in the thirteenth round.

Billy Brierley, from a Liverpool family of boxing brothers and hailed as the bantam champion of Lancashire, was the next man in the ring with George. Brierley, only nineteen to George's twenty-one, was considered a good test for the Sheffielder and 'the battle of the roses' captured the city's imagination, resulting in a big crowd at the Drill Hall. George's form continued and he celebrated a comfortable points win.

The young boxer's growth in stature in the boxing world earned him his biggest pay night so far and his stiffest opponent. He was matched with 'Chappie' Moran in a fight for £200 at the Drill Hall in December 1893. Michael Moran, born in the Midlands of Irish parentage, had learned his craft in America.

Six years previously in Jersey City he had won the American bantam championship. He had defended the title successfully the following year, and returned to England where he beat some of the best men in the country, before going back to America. While in the States, he had fought Tommy Kelly and was unlucky to lose. In fact, Kelly, who had laid claim to the World Bantam Title in 1892 (the champion George Dixon had moved to featherweight and relinquished his title, Kelly claimed the title because he had drawn with Dixon) had refused to fight Moran again, and Kelly outweighed Moran by a stone. It has to be remembered that flyweight, which was Moran and Corfield's real weight, did not come into being until 1909.

It was a hard fight for George and very much a tale of two halves. For the first ten rounds he had the best of the fight, his telling left proving most effective. In the second half of the fight, the more experienced Moran forced his way back into the reckoning, and although George was able to hang on and complete his points victory, Moran had made a sorry mess of his eyes. The victory over such a worthy opponent signalled Corfield's arrival in the top class of his weight.

After George's next victory at the Drill Hall, against Bill Moore of London, he was matched with another Londoner, Alf Gower in September 1894 for the 7 stone 12lb championship.

The bantam limit at that time was eight stone. Incidentally, eight stone is now the flyweight limit, the bantam limit having risen to 8 stone 4lb. Billy Plimmer was the bantam champion, so unofficially there was no title division under that weight. The promoters, on bringing the best two men together at 7 stone 7lb, gave the fight the championship tag and, in fact, the publicity freely called it a World Title fight. If there had been rankings in this period, Corfield had proved worthy of the occasion with his defeat of Moran, while Gower, a big favourite at the National Sporting Club, was considered the top man at 7 stone 12lb, south of Sheffield.

Norfolk Drill Hall drew a full house to see the local man in his bid for championship honours. George didn't let them down and to thunderous applause, his explosive punching created so much havoc that Gower had to retire with a broken jaw, his seconds terminating the Londoner's challenge before the thirteenth round commenced.

As Sheffield rejoiced in the acknowledgement of their champion, George stated that next on his agenda was a match with Billy Plimmer. Plimmer had become British bantam champion in 1891, but since then he had fought mostly in America. He had knocked out Tommy Kelly in 1892 who had claimed the world title after George Dixon had relinquished it, and to put the issue that he was a World bantam champion beyond doubt, he had beaten Dixon at catch-weight and Dixon was World Featherweight Champion.

Sheffield businessman, Horace Bee, had become Corfield's biggest backer and another Bee associate, R. Ford, his manager. The demand was so big to get George a match with Plimmer that negotiations were conducted while the champion was still in America. Bee would have preferred the fight in Sheffield, the scene of all George's triumphs, but as the National Sporting Club in London was the order of the day for title fights, Plimmer's backers were able to call the tune, especially as the champion had refused to box in Sheffield. Before the fight, Plimmer arrived in Sheffield and the local fans were able to witness the man their hero was fighting in a two day boxing carnival at Quaglienis Circus in Matilda Street, promoted by Plimmer and his brother.

In May 1895, in a match arranged for £880 and the title 7 stone 12lb Championship of the World, George stepped into the ring at the National Sporting Club. The fight being the first time George had fought outside Sheffield. After arriving in the capital, it was found that George was over the specified weight and although he weighed in at 7 stone 10 and a half pounds, he had, in fact, lost four pounds in the two days before the fight. Disappointingly George was well below par and Plimmer, who forced the fighting throughout, easily beat him in seven rounds.

Desperate to prove himself in the top flight after his London appearance, George met Nunc Wallace at Norfolk Drill Hall in September 1895. Sheffield's boxing fraternity hadn't lost their faith in him and one thousand people crowded the hall to see their hero resume his boxing career. Former knuckle fighter Wallace had fought for the World Bantam Title in 1890 and had been stopped by George Dixon.

George's left coolly banged away and by the fifth round Wallace's nose was bleeding. The Sheffielder easily met Wallace's wild rushes and it surprised the onlookers that he lasted as long as the eighteenth round.

George's next venture was to open his own boxing school, 'the Excelsior School of Arms' at Furnace Hill. Although the premises were rather small for big promotions, George was a popular figure at the open competitions held there, often officiating as either MC or referee and was also at hand to donate prizes to the novices.

It was from a Sheffield novice that the next challenge to Corfield came. Harry Maurier, who had never taken part in a stake match, had argued that Corfield could not concede him six pounds in weight. George duly accepted the challenge and a match was made for £100 at 8 stone 6lb at Rotherham.

It proved a hell of a fight and Maurier showed he was no novice and gave George more punishment than in any of his previous encounters. Class finally told, but Corfield's points victory was close.

High upon George's list was a rematch with Plimmer. In their earlier meeting George had thought he had let the Sheffield people down and to help erase the memory, a return was sought with the great boxer. Plimmer had, in fact, lost his World title on a disqualification to Pedlar Palmer 'the Box of Tricks' in late 1895.

The return between George and Plimmer took place in September 1896, and this time Plimmer was willing to come to Sheffield. It is doubtful whether a fight has ever created so much interest in Sheffield as the rematch did. Crowds lined the way to the Drill Hall to see the boxers arrive for action, in a fight arranged for the huge purse of £1,400. In front of his own supporters, George put up a great show and the fight lived up to every expectation. Billy Plimmer was a master boxer and he proved that to the Sheffield audience who, although their hearts were with the local man who fought the fight of his life, were ready to acknowledge Plimmer's victory after the twenty round battle.

Beaten, but not disgraced, Sheffield's boxing idol was full of praise for Plimmer's brilliance. It is doubtful whether anyone could have beaten Plimmer that night as he showed completely why he had been World champion. The winner was so delighted by his reception that he resided in Sheffield afterwards, and the great battle lived on a long while in the locals' minds.

The fight also lived on for another reason. Jem Carney, who had been Plimmer's second, had advanced £500, the amount of the sidestake. It was generally understood that if Plimmer had won, the £500 would be returned and if he lost, it was not expected. The affair ended as a court case to hear the Court of Appeal decide the question of whether a loan to a principal in a prize fight was recoverable under the gaming act.

The two fights with Plimmer were the pick of George Corfield's career. There were other fights; he became a stumbling block to many of the up and coming aspiring champions, including the northern champion, Paddy Mahoney at Stalybridge in 1897. He was still a fixture in Sheffield boxing promotions during the period of the First World War. Tommy Gummer recalled him being employed as a timekeeper at Carbrook when he fought Gus Platts. Now largely forgotten, his boxing ability gave him the right to the title 'Sheffield's first boxing idol'.

'IRON' HAGUE

S outh Yorkshire's first British Championship holder was Mexborough's own William 'Iron' Hague who knocked out the champion, Gunner Moir, in the first round to take the heavyweight title in 1909.

He began developing his strong boy 'Iron' reputation at school and it was said he was insensitive to pain and thought nothing of punching brick walls!

By the time he was fifteen in 1900, his local reputation had grown and he was visiting local fairs pitting his strength in the boxing booths. His early efforts earned him a ten shilling note for standing up to a notable local boxer, Tommy Stokes, and a gold sovereign for putting away another so called booth expert.

After leaving his first job in the glassworks, the young Hague went to work in the pits, but that job wasn't held long. Teaming up with Jim Watson, a coloured boxer from Leeds, 'Iron' began to make his name as a boxer whose strength and punching power were his greatest assets.

Turning professional at eighteen, 'Iron' had his first fight at Doncaster Drill Hall against Don Lewis, punching his opponent out of the ring in the sixth round. Fighting mostly in South Yorkshire, the Mexborough boy soon proved a hit with both spectators and opponents' chins.

Now appearing as a heavyweight, 'Iron' had an enormous appetite, which had shot his weight up to fourteen stone. He also found that his growing reputation made it harder to get opponents into the ring, and there were often lengthy periods between fights.

In 1908 in Sheffield, 'Iron' was matched with Frank Craig, better known as 'the Harlem Coffee Cooler'. Although only a middleweight and near the end of his career, Craig, an American negro, had campaigned successfully all over the world and ten years previously had won the British middleweight title, although he wasn't officially recognised.

Nevertheless he was still a big name in boxing and 'Iron's' four round win attracted the attention of London promoters.

The turning point, which was to make him a national figure in boxing, came when he was given the chance to appear in a novice's heavyweight competition at the National Sporting Club. 'Iron's'

'Iron' Hague British Heavyweight Champion, 1910-11.   *(Photo loaned by Bill Matthews)*.

explosive punching made short work of the other entrants and the door was open for more appearances at boxing's headquarters.

In Derby week the same year, he made his second appearance at the club against Corporal Sunshine, an experienced boxer and services heavyweight champion. Not worried about reputations,

'Iron' beat his opponent in four rounds. His next foe, Charlie Wilson of Notting Hill, went the same way - down and out in four rounds. Promoters thought that they had got the right opponent for the Yorkshireman when he was matched with Big Ben Taylor, the 'Woolwich Infant'.

Hague was finding it difficult in keeping his weight down between fights but Taylor outweighed him by a stone. A spectacular second round knockout, after Taylor had picked himself up off the floor three times, led the London promoters to believe that Hague was the right man to challenge for the heavyweight title held by Gunner James Moir.

British champion since October 1906, Gunner had been given the chance to fight for the world title against the visiting Tommy Burns. Easily beaten in ten rounds by the world champion, Moir had been inactive in the eighteen months since the fight, earning money on the music hall circuit as a vaudeville performer.

After 'Iron' was nominated as the official challenger, Moir was called upon by the Sporting Club to defend his title over twenty rounds.

The fight made headlines in South Yorkshire and 'Iron's' supporters helped to raise the £300 sidestake which, with the £900 purse (£600 winner, loser £300), made the fight for those times a big money match. In April 1909, 'Iron' stepped into the ring at the NSCC to challenge for the British heavyweight title. Instead of lasting for twenty rounds, the fight was over before the bell had gone for the end first! The Mexborough giant had won the title at the first attempt and in the first round. During the First World War, Charlie Hardcastle achieved the same feat. Moir, who was seven years the senior, was flat on his back, floored by Hague's explosive punching.

England welcomed a new heavyweight champion and indeed a new 'white hope'. Immediately there was talk of him facing the new world champion, Jack Johnson, who, after beating Burns in Australia, had returned to America. The National Sporting Club had financed his trip to Australia on the understanding that, if he won, he would return to England to fight his great rival, Sam Langford. Johnson had been given a hard time by Langford in their only fight and the new champion had no intention of granting the 'Boston Tar Baby' a return bout. Seeing that Langford was already in the country, it was obvious to put him in with the new British champion.

It was well-known that 'Iron's' hobbies outside the ring were drinking beer, eating and sleeping. Training, to him, was an evil. His new found fame as champion had made him a popular man and as his social life extended, his training was put into the background.

Despite warnings, 'Iron' thought that all the training he needed was in the ring with his opponents and his strength and punching power would see him through. 'Peggy' Bettinson, manager at the Sporting Club, told the story that shortly before the scheduled date, he went to see Hague in training and found him indulging in his usual 'beer and skittles'. He warned him he had better look to his condition in his forthcoming fight. 'Why?' asked 'Iron'. 'He doesn't weigh twelve stone. Whatever chance has a man of that weight got with me?'.

Langford, only 5ft 6in tall and really only a middleweight, had spent most of his career fighting heavies and wasn't alarmed at fighting a much taller and heavier man. Langford's record was eighty-nine fights with only six losses and he was the only man to have put Johnson on the floor. 'Iron's' fights, even though he was about the same age, numbered less than a quarter of Langford's.

The American was paid £2,500 for the fight and if a story that circulated later in America is true, his manager, Joe Woodman, after hearing tales of 'Iron's' condition, was so confident that he put the full amount on the result with a London bookie only minutes before the fight took place. Special guest at the ringside was a former champion, Bob Fitzsimmons, holder in his time of three world titles and a man who had spent most of his career fighting heavier men.

'Iron's' younger brother, Johnny, was also on the bill and his performance in beating his fellow Yorkshireman, Tim Woodward, added spice to the top of the bill fight. It was generally accepted that the bout was to go on for a time for the benefit of filmmaking. 'Iron's' out for the kill attitude completely destroyed the arrangement. He instantly set about Langford and caught him with a second round swing, putting him on the canvas. According to the contemporary descriptions of the blow, which landed on Langford's ear, it was so powerful that Langford turned a full cartwheel in the ring. The packed house was in uproar. Could the seemingly out of condition Hague pull off a surprise and whip the fancied American? At the end of the round, Langford leaned over to his manager: 'Say Joe! There ain't going to be no pictures'. Langford produced the fireworks in the fourth round. A flurry of rights and Hague went down pole-axed, and as the seconds tried to revive him, Langford leaned over to the side, with a big grin on his face, exclaiming: 'That baby's out for keeps!'. When he came round, Iron couldn't believe that the smaller man had beaten him. The American had proved that strength and punching power were not enough.

After the defeat, 'Iron' returned home to Mexborough, basing himself at the *Montagu Hotel*, where his backer, F.J. Law, was owner, under his trainer Charlie Bolton. Charlie was known to his intimates as the noted ploughboy from Barmbro' and adviser George Lew.

In the next two years or so he had eight fights, losing three, but as these fights were fought outside the jurisdiction of the Sporting Club, his victors were not recognised as champions and 'Iron' continued to claim the title. On the undercard of the Spike Robson versus Jim Driscoll featherweight title fight, Hague, who was now up to fifteen stone, met the giant 6ft 3in tall Bill Chase from Forest Gate at the Sporting Club. Chase was really an unknown. His only claim to fame was the winning of a novice's competition.

A butcher by trade, Chase wasn't in the fight to the fifth round when a hard left to the jaw annexed Hague. He was quickly on one knee and rose at the count of eight. As Chase came in for the kill, Hague met him full on, wading in with both hands and before the audience could grasp the situation, the roles were reversed. Chase was finished and he was carried to his corner, a victim of 'Iron's' explosive hitting.

There was one match which Hague wanted to win and that was against Jewey Smith from London. Smith came to Sheffield not long after 'Iron's' title win and beat the local hero on points at the Carver Street Club. Ten months later 'Iron' and Smith met again at the Attercliffe Hall and the fact that Hague had actually trained for the fight made all the difference. It was another hard fight as the two rivals slugged it out, but after the twenty rounds, 'Iron' had his revenge by not too large a margin of points.

The Olympic Rink at Mexborough provided the setting for 'Iron's' match with Sergeant Sunshine of the Royal Fusiliers. 'Iron's' strength proving too much for the Sergeant, Sunshine going down in round nine.

There was another victory over an army man when an eighteen round win over Corporal Brown of the 3rd Grenadier Guards was recorded.

In 1911, 'Iron' was matched with Bombadier Billy Wells at the National Sporting Club for 'Iron's' titles. Wells had been the champion of India in 1909 and on his return to England, he quickly won a reputation as a knockout specialist. A defeat by Gunner Moir, whom 'Iron' had humiliated in one round, led Hague's backers to think he was there for the taking.

When the club announced that the first Lonsdale Belt for competition in the heavyweight division would be presented to the winner, 'Iron' even trained for the fight and was half a stone lighter than his weight for the Langford fight two years earlier.

The fight produced six punishing rounds in which Wells withstood 'Iron's' hardest punches. Two long counts in the fourth round and a third in the sixth was the finish of Hague. This was his last big fight.

The Mexborough battler became a First World War casualty, returning home gassed. He never left the area and lived at Harlington Road, Mexborough working, amongst other jobs, at Steel, Peach and Tozer.

Frankie Round, a later Mexborough boxer, once told me a tale about 'Iron' Hague, which was very characteristic of the man. Frankie was courting 'Iron's' daughter and on first introduction to the man who had been his schoolboy idol, the former champion greeted the youngster with 'They tell me you're gonna be a boxer son'. 'Yes, Mr Hague', replied the eager to please Frankie. 'Do you know what a straight left is?' returned 'Iron'. Before Frankie had even a chance to consider the question, 'Iron' showed him exactly what a straight left was, leaving the young boxer the victim of his first knockout.

Judged purely on his skill as a boxer, 'Iron' Hague wasn't a great by any stretch of the imagination, but as a strong man with punching power, certainly this country hasn't seen many equals.

Scott Welch, holder of Hague's old title during 1995-96 unveils a plaque to the former champion in Mexborough. *(Photo loaned by Giles Brearley).*

CHARLIE HARDCASTLE

There has only been one Barnsley born lad to win a British title and that was Charlie Hardcastle, the fighting miner. The first four letters of his surname were no joke, because that's what he was, one of the hardest hitters to come from the featherweight ranks. Charlie holds a rare record along with very few other boxing greats and that is he won his title at the first attempt and in the first round.

Boxing was only a hobby in his early days, being strictly a recreation following his shift in the pit.

Charlie came to know about a competition held in the area, open to all comers for the 8 stone 6lb championship title of Yorkshire, to be held at the Sheffield Boxing Club in Carver Street. The City Boxing Club, like many other clubs in the early years of the century leading up to the First World War, ran open competitions for various Yorkshire titles. There was no official recognition for any of the titles. Promoters in the major towns throughout the country were also running similar open title contests. These competitions were the kind of break a youngster needed if he was striving to make good.

Gus Platts also fought in similar competitions at the same time and when he wrote his memoirs, he remembered some of them very well for the simple reason that he didn't get paid. Out of the sixteen or so entrants, quite often only the finalists were paid, often only with a medal. So ideally in the promoter's eyes, on the first round bill with eight

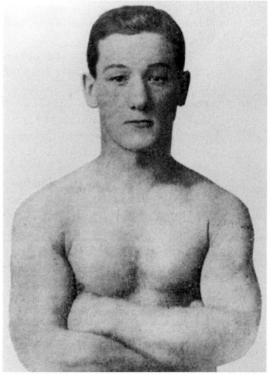

Charlie Hardcastle, the Barnsley pitman. British Featherweight Champion 1917. *(Photo loaned by Bill Matthews).*

fights, there was little or nothing to pay out.

In the event which Charlie entered, he met Joe Fletcher from Sheffield in the first round of bouts and finished him in two rounds. In the next round Arthur Bullivant, another lad from the steel city, retired at the end of the third after taking enough punishment from Charlie. In the semi-final Charlie met Walter Holden, the favourite for the title. Once again, the hard-hitting Barnsley boy outpunched his rival, with Holden retiring after four rounds. The final was between Lewis Ruddick already well-known in Leeds and Charlie, the 'Barnsley Bombshell'.

There is some doubt that the actual final took place. I have heard of other finals that didn't happen so it is possible that this didn't. Boxing historian Gilbert Odd, who wrote a couple of articles that mentioned Charlie, failed to trace any record and after conversation with the now late and very helpful Mr Odd, I spent some time looking through local papers which failed to clear up the mystery. However Ruddick and Hardcastle did meet a few times on future occasions, these fights producing a couple of draws and verdicts for both men.

The next big event for Charlie was the winning of the pitmen's championship at nine stone, which he won by knocking out Billy Green of Chesterfield at the Barnsley Empire. It was only then that his boxing was taken seriously, and the road to the top started to open up.

The National Sporting Club, headquarters of British boxing was the next stop and it was a headlining start. Hardcastle's opponent was Londoner, Mike Honeyman, who was a good few years younger, but very experienced. Charlie's explosive hitting had Honeyman down in the first round and by the second round it was all over. His punching ability, if not his boxing skill, impressed the members and Charlie was invited back on several subsequent occasions. Honeyman's turn was to come later and he eventually became champion three years after Charlie.

London visits between pit shifts became regular ocurrences and Charlie developed into a major attraction with his early round finishes. Ben Clarke of Portsmouth was seen off in one round, Joe Starmer from Kettering lasted three and Young Lippo from Portsmouth went in eight rounds. Londoner Bob Cotton spoilt the record by going fourteen rounds and eventually knocking Charlie out. Cotton had been down several times for counts, but had weathered the storm. Unused to going so long in a fight, Charlie tired and the refreshed Cotton caught him and sent him to the canvas.

Lack of real training was one of the reasons for Charlie's failure to last the pace.

Arthur Cooper, a Barnsley man, took him in hand and for the first time Hardcastle began to take his training and the sport seriously. The big right hand was well-known, now there was a development of the left and speed was added to his all-round fighting combination.

Charlie's fight with Louis Hood, a sapper in the army, ended with a right-hander, but with the worst possible outcome. Hood failed to regain consciousness and tragically died the next day. Charlie was taken to Bow Street and charged with manslaughter. However an inquest verdict of death by misadventure was returned and he was released. Ring deaths affect different boxers in different ways. Charlie returned home shattered and vowed never to enter the ring again. Within a month he was persuaded to resume but it was obvious the tragedy was still playing on his mind. His next three fights all

went the distance. Curley Walker and Arthur Hayes both beat the Barnsley man while Charlie beat Young Brooks on points.

During 1916, the Welshman Llew Edwards relinquished his British title. The featherweight champion had been in Australia for over a year and had started to box as a lightweight. A series of eliminators was arranged for the vacant title and Charlie met Welshman, Billy Fanner. Charlie was now under Jack Goodwin, a London trainer of some standing. Goodwin's influence was enough to restore Charlie's aggression with the result that his punches were not held back and Fanner was beaten in seven rounds.

Charlie was matched with Londoner, Alf Wye, for the vacant title in 1917. Wye had been the ABA bantam title-holder before becoming a professional and over the last year Alf had completed four victorious bouts at the Sporting Club. Among Wye's victories were Curly Walker, the former bantam champion and Cotton, both winners over Hardcastle. Wye's form made him the 7-4 favourite.

In order to have leave from the pit for preparation, Charlie worked a couple of double shifts.

It was eleven o'clock at night when on Monday 4 June 1917, Charlie entered the ring to meet the lighter, taller challenger. By three minutes past, the MC was announcing the new British featherweight champion. The contest was brief and sensational, for before the first round bell had sounded, Charlie had knocked Wye out. Instead of the big right, it was the left that floored Wye, knocking him clean out.

After staying the night in the capital, Hardcastle was greeted by hordes of fans at Barnsley station on his return. But the next day it was back to work in the colliery.

Charlie's first engagement as champion was a month later at Holborne Stadium against an old foe, the little Leeds battler. Louis Ruddick. It is debatable whether the Barnsley man was as fit as he had been the month before. Clinching was the main feature of the early rounds, referee Eugene Corri repeatedly breaking the two fighters apart. Corri's voice dominated the fight throughout, warning Ruddick several times about his head. The Leeds man was the boxer to land clean punches and they were sparse. Hardcastle tired very quickly and it was a case of the collier hanging on as his legs started to go. After fourteen rounds had been completed of the scheduled fifteen, in what had been for the spectators a very uninteresting affair, the last round brought fireworks.

It was very apparent that Charlie's strength had given out. Seeing his chance, Ruddick discarded his previous style and went all out to win by hard knocks in open fighting. Three times he sent Hardcastle to the floor, but apparently in his excitement he struck one blow when the man was technically down. His victory seemed to be taken for granted by the spectators who had naturally become worked up to a state of high excitement. Some seconds elapsed before a hearing could be obtained and then it was given out from the stage that Ruddick had been disqualified.

After his lucky win over Ruddick, Charlie was matched against Tancy Lee in his first defence of his featherweight title. Lee had won the British and European flyweight titles in 1915 and had surprised the boxing world by beating the invincible Jimmy Wilde in the process.

The thirty-six-year-old Scot had stepped up in weight. He had won the Scottish bantam title and was now challenging for the British Featherweight title. Five months after the Wye match, Charlie stepped into the ring with Lee at the National Sporting Club. The nine years older Scot was the 7-4 favourite, being the only man at that moment in time to have beaten Wilde and the only British man to do so, this obviously enhancing his reputation.

A certain amount of clinching marred the first round and in the opening rounds, despite the tendency to hold, Charlie's form was the better. Some heavy blows were exchanged and Lee took a clear lead. In the fourth round, the match was unexpectedly over. Hardcastle rallied and Lee backed off to draw the Yorkshireman into his trap. A right uppercut lifted the champion clear off his feet and the ten second count was a mere formality.

With Lee the new champion, Hardcastle returned to his job in the pit and it was a while before his boxing career was resumed.

This marked the end of Charlie's reign in the top flight. He continued to fight for the next seven years or so, but his early form was never recaptured and there were plenty of defeats. During his sixty-six fight career, Charlie won thirty-eight and lost twenty.

He fought Salford's Billy Marchant three times, losing twice and drawing once and there were three memorable scraps with Sheffield's Tommy Gray. Charlie won the first two, one of which at Barnsley Drill Hall was very close. The third meeting at a W. Downes' promotion at Edmund Road Drill Hall proved to be Tommy's revenge. During the ninth round Charlie fell pole-axed to a double combination and indeed it was some considerable time before he was revived.

Not long after this bout Charlie retired, but he was still active in Barnsley boxing circles for some time and was a frequent visitor giving advice to up and coming youngsters at Fred Holden's gym.

TOMMY GUMMER

O ne of the highlights of my boxing research came in 1980 when I went to visit Tommy Gummer at Rotherham while compiling a series for the *Sheffield Star*. Tommy, at the time was eighty-five, and was Britain's oldest living champion and had not long returned from London where he had travelled to attend the Boxing Board's 50th anniversary dinner.

Tommy's memory was as fresh as if he was recalling events from a few weeks ago and although I had previously carefully researched his career, Tommy needed not the slightest prompting. What a distinct pleasure it was talking with someone who had actually boxed before the First World War and who had first hand experience of some of the greatest boxers who had ever lived. Not long after the interview, possibly the last he ever gave, the remarkable ex-champion passed away.

Born in Kimberworth in 1894, the second son of a family of five, Tommy's first lesson in the finer art was from his elder brother Richard, who eventually became welterweight champion of the Mediterranean Fleet. After his father had died when he was only eight, Tommy left school at thirteen to go down the nearby pit at Droppingwell. Joining the local amateur club, the Don Athletic, he soon showed promise by winning a nine stone competition. Tommy recalled in this period visiting the local fair at Wincobank where he disposed of the booth's champion in one round and was barred from entering the ring again until the following day when he met the booth's owner in an exhibition, earning a couple of shillings for his trouble.

Putting on weight, he travelled to Carlton Hall Barracks, Leeds in 1913 to enter a 'white hope' competition. Promoted by the *Daily Sketch* and *Sporting Chronicle*, the plan was to hold a series of similar contests in each county and then match the winners in a series of heats to find a challenger for the British Heavyweight title at the National Sporting Club. The phrase 'white hope', was coined during coloured boxer Jack Johnson's dominance of the world title.

Tommy's weight at the time was only in the eleven and a half stone region, but nevertheless he proved the winner among the sixteen entrants, coming away with £10 and a gold medal. His performance in the first round when he made his opponent unconscious, so

frightened his second opponent, he quit before a punch had been thrown. Tommy clinched the final with a three round knockout victory.

The following year, Tommy turned professional making his debut in Liverpool, where he fought on the Bandsman Rice versus Bombadier Wells bill, commencing with a six round win over Willie Monks, who incidentally had won the Lancashire 'White Hope' competition, the original competition was cancelled due to the outbreak of war, at which time Tommy joined the 5th Battalion of the Lancashire and Yorkshire Regiment and within a year had risen to the rank of sergeant.

Bouts were made available and Tommy began to make a name for himself. Fighting in the open-air stadium at Carbrook Fields Sheffield , behind the *Pheasant Inn*, Tommy became a local favourite and several inside the distance wins made his name prominent and he was soon in demand from other promoters.

In 1915 he was matched against Mexborough's 'Iron' Hague. Although past his best, Hague had been the British heavyweight champion in 1909 and was very much a local hero. Tommy had, indeed, watched him fight only two years previously, never thinking that in less than two years he would be meeting him in the ring. Knocking him out in ten rounds, the much lighter Tommy was immediately matched with another local idol, Gus Platts.

Creating plenty of local interest (Tommy had wisely taken the Hague and Platts fights on percentages), the fight with Gus had the fans in uproar. In the ninth round the Kimberworth lad floored Platts six times, but surprisingly this didn't do enough to win the fight. In spite of the counts, the referee gave the verdict to Gus after he had hung on throughout the tenth as Tommy failed to land the knockout blow. Tommy was indeed upset at this setback, especially as several first hand witnesses had exclaimed that some of the ninth round counts had been overlong. Even the local paper had noticed a similar feeling as their report told of over generous counts.

Still fighting heavier men, he made his National Sporting Club debut and was beaten in five rounds by Harry Curzon. Staying in London, Tommy made several appearances in 'The Ring', Blackfriars, and among the opponents he beat were Louis Verger from Switzerland, Tim Warner, the army heavyweight champion and Sid Burns, father of the 1950s promoter Sam Burns.

Ted Broadribb, a former boxer under the nickname of 'Young Snowball' and due later to become famous as the manager of Freddie Mills, wrote to Tommy while he was in the army offering to become his manager. The arrangement didn't work out too satisfactory for when Tommy was able to get leave from the army he was involved in a series of mismatches. In his second National Sporting Club appearance, the heavier Frank Goddard, a future British heavyweight champion, knocked him out. Coming out of his sick-bed he was still in his 'hospital blues' pyjamas and lost two fights in a week. Harry Curzon beat him for a second time and Liverpool's Arthur Townley proved too strong for Gummer.

Tommy lost a third fight shortly after at Newcastle against Frank Ray.

In July 1917, Sergeant Gummer was duly drafted to France. Twice wounded in action Tommy distinguished himself by winning the Military Medal for gallantry in the field. Thus, the war had put the Rotherham lad out of action and it was after a lengthy period of convalescence that his ring career was eventually resumed. After his recuperation, Tommy began his comeback with another tilt at Harry Curzon and, at the third time of trying, stopped him in the eighteenth round at Hoxton Baths. At the 'Ring' he beat Belgian, Henry Tynke who, strangely, was a member of the Australian armed forces, winning in the twentieth round despite taking several counts.

When the return bout was set at 11 stone 6lb, the limit for a middleweight Tommy, realising that he was able to make the weight after spending all his career fighting 'heavies' and 'cruisers', decided to become a serious challenger as a middleweight. After winning the return, a match was fixed at the Sporting Club, hopefully for the middleweight title. The title was vacant at that time. Pat O'Keefe, who had been champion on and off for twelve years, had finally relinquished his title, after winning his Lonsdale Belt outright.

When Boy McCormick, Gummer's opponent, weighed in he was over a stone heavier but the fight still went ahead as a catchweight contest. Despite giving his best, Tommy was beaten in twelve rounds. McCormick showed his class by also winning the light heavyweight title two months later in only his thirteenth professional fight.

After working overtime to gain a hard earned twenty round draw with Jim Harris at the 'Ring' on a Monday night, his manager booked Tommy to fight American, Eddie McGoorty, at Dublin on the Thursday. Completely worn out, he was beaten in two rounds. McGoorty, who was a world title claimant, was clearly in a different class.

Understandably dissatisfied with Broadribb as his trainer, Tommy decided to manage his own affairs and after winning his last fight under Broadribb's management, destroying Fred Rhye in three rounds at the Sporting Club, Tommy went back home to South Yorkshire.

Back at Carbrook, under promoters Whitham and Salt, he outpointed his old rival Curzon.

Now Tommy was back on home ground, high on his list was a rematch with Sheffield's Gus Platts. Since their early fight at the beginning of the war, both fighters had reached the top in the middleweight field. A local derby between the Rotherham and the

Sheffield man was a natural choice and the fight was duly arranged at Sheffield City Hall. Revenge was sweet for Tommy; he had felt cheated at their earlier meeting. This time he made no mistake and outpunched Platts to earn a fifteen round points win.

The National Sporting Club duly noted the win and as the middleweight title was still vacant, Tommy was matched with Jim Sullivan for the title at the club in March 1920. Sullivan, from Bermondsey, had been champion in 1910, but had given up his title to try his luck in Australia. Since the war, Sullivan had hardly fought, averaging only about one fight a year for the last four years and he had not fought competitively since 1918. Since he was the younger man by eight years, there was an air of confidence in the Gummer camp. Despite rival promoters' attempts to break the Sporting Club's hold on all the title contests, the bout was given official standing by the awarding of a new Lonsdale trophy.

A fortnight before the Gummer versus Sullivan fight, promoter Charles B. Cochran, trying to steal one over on the NSC matched Ted Kid Lewis (dubbed the 'smashing, dashing, crashing Kid', Lewis had been British and European featherweight champion and was current world welterweight champion, and would go on to fight in a staggering forty-two title fights), against Johnny Bee of Birkenhead in a fight advertised as for the British Middleweight title and for a bigger purse than Tommy's fight.

Lewis beat Bee in four rounds, but despite Cochran's claims, Tommy's fight with Sullivan was the official pairing.

Up to the back end of the fight, the scoring was about even, then in the twelfth round, Sullivan had Tommy in trouble, but was unable to nail him. During the fourteenth, Tommy hastened by the fact he was probably losing on points, cut loose and Sullivan took several counts. The towel came in from Sullivan's corner and Yorkshire had another British title under its belt. Returning to the traditional homecoming reserved for all champions, Tommy decided his first fight as champion would be at Carbrook, against former middleweight champion Bandsman Blake. Celebrating in style, he beat Blake inside a round. His next two opponents were Herbert Crossley, the ill-fated Mexborough light heavyweight and Fred Stanley.

His fight with the heavier Crossley produced a draw whilst his bout with Stanley was stopped in the thirteenth round with Gummer clearly ahead. It was revealed later that during the Stanley fight, Tommy had broken his hand and although he still had more fights to come, the injury seriously hampered him and eventually forced him to retire.

When a chance came to fight Ercole Balzac, the French champion, for the vacant European middleweight title, Tommy travelled to the newly opened Sporting Club de Paris. Despite good work in the early rounds, the rugged Frenchman wore him down and Tommy was finished in the ninth round. Two months later, Balzac travelled to Yorkshire to meet Gus Platts and the Sheffield lad sent him home without his titles.

The scene was now set for a decider between Platts and Gummer. Knowing this was to be his last fight because of a suspect hand, Tommy agreed that it should be for both titles, although because the fight was out of the NSC jurisdiction, if Platts won the club would not recognise him as champion.

The Drill Hall was packed to the rafters to see the two rivals decide their third clash, the honours so far being even. Tommy's hand went again and Gus was able to beat him in six rounds to claim the British title to go along with his European crown. Now announcing his retirement officially and returning the Lonsdale Belt to London, Tommy was content to take a back seat. But as we all know, old fighters don't lie down and fifteen months later he was persuaded to take on Ted Kid Lewis. By now Lewis was the official British and European middleweight champion and had even claimed the British light heavyweight title after knocking out Boy McCormick. When Tommy had been champion, Lewis had criticised him for wanting too much money for a middleweight unification match and although a match was made at 11 stone 6lb, Tommy weighed in over the weight. Morton Lewis in his biography on his father *Ted Kid Lewis - His Life and Times*, stated he was up to as much as 13 stone 10lb, though Tommy didn't agree with that.

In the only regret of his boxing career, Tommy was beaten inside a round after making himself weak trying to get down to championship weight.

After retiring for the second time, Tommy became a referee and was the third man in the ring for a number of years. His boxing interest never waned and in his later years he was a keen member of the Sheffield Old Boxers' Association.

Gus Platts

THE CHIEF CANDIDATE for the title of Mr Boxing in Sheffield during the boom era of the 1920s and 1930s was Augustus T. Platts, more commonly known as Gus Platts. His lengthy career encompassed over 200 fights and saw him at his peak as European middleweight champion and this was followed by a period in management and promotion at several venues.

Gus was born at Heavygate Road, Walkley in 1891. His first interest wasn't in boxing but physical culture, a craze which was at its height around the turn of the century. His interest in boxing was a relatively late development. Joining the Stanley Street Physical Culture Club as a youngster, his first proud moment was when he won a health and strength competition. Wrestling was an interest in the formative years of Gus Platts, his heroes being those two great international wrestling stars Hackenschmidt and Yokio Tani. When a young fellow from East Ardsley threw out a challenge to anyone under eighteen years at eight stone, the young Sheffielder took up his challenge. Despite trouble from a tooth extraction earlier in the day, Gus had a comfortable win at the Comrades Hall. His wrestling career lasted about twenty bouts, of which he never lost one. In his later memory, the outstanding bout was a match against a Treeton lad in 1908, in which he gained his first cauliflower ear.

George Flood who ran the boxing at the club and who himself promoted boxing shows all around the South Yorkshire belt, was one of the first men to persuade Gus to don the boxing gloves. Flood, along with a neighbour of Gus, Billy Hughes, persuaded young Platts to enter one of George Dinney's open competitions at Attercliffe *Theatre Royal*. Their faith was justified and Gus easily reached the final which, unfortunately, didn't take place. When the Platts family moved to Upperthorpe, where Gus trained in the attic, his father brought home some of his Sunday afternoon drinking pals to watch the lad work out. Mrs Platts kicked the lot out. 'No boxing on Sunday in this house' she argued, and the party had to arrange a later show down at the *Hallamshire Hotel*.

Billy Hughes then took him to Bradford to enter a nine stone amateur competition. Gus again reached the final, beating on the way another pro-boxer in the making, Kid Eastwood of Brighouse.

Gus Platts, Sheffield's Mr Boxing. (*Photo loaned by Bill Matthews*).

His lack of experience let him down in the final and Jim Long of Leeds (who Gus learned later was a bogus amateur), gave him a 'terrible pasting', which the referee finally stopped. This defeat didn't deter Gus' new found ambition to become a professional boxer and it wasn't long after a series of sparring sessions at the *Adelphi* with South African Arthur Ellis, that Platts made his professional debut.

His first paid contest was at the new City Boxing Club, Carver Street, Sheffield. Arthur Ellis was the referee.

The fight was a bottom of the bill ten rounder against Albert Woodhouse and took place on 8 August 1910, the week following bank holiday. As Gus and Albert wanted some pocket money for Cleethorpes, they subbed 8s each and fought the week after for a 'paltry four bob' (the fight being arranged at a £1 12s winner, 8s loser). Gus, who was billed as the 'unbeaten local wrestling champion', stopped Woodhouse in the fourth round.

Young Platts was soon in action again when, at Attercliffe Hall on a Jack Whitham, Alf Axe and Bankes promotion, he knocked out Attercliffe boy Jack Frith in the third round. After a 'demolition job' on George Lewis at the same venue, Gus soared to the top of the Thursday night shows at Attercliffe.

Gus related an interesting story of his novice days in an article in the *Sheffield Telegraph* in 1922.

'Alf Axe took me to see a fight at Rotherham. It was in a dirty, small room, with a low ceiling, and reeking of the fumes from a suspended oil lamp. The ring was on the floor in this terrible place, and there was a rare motley crowd present. I can remember the feeling of loathing I had on entering, little did I think I was in for such a night of excitement! "He'll fight anybody in Yorkshire at nine stone" quoth Axe, referring to yours truly and straightaway a big brawny fellow named Jack Bentley with slouch cap, muffler and cigarette in the corner of his mouth, dived through the ropes and said 'I'm his man!' So we were fixed up for ten rounds the following week.

I was giving a lot of weight away, my feelings when I saw the great giant in the opposite corner can be imagined. 'Can I get him down, I wonder?' Went through my brains a dozen times. It didn't take me long to find out. Oh, I hit that fellow with both hands until I was fairly sick of it. I knocked him from pillar to post and landed the finishing punch in round six. They carried him home unconscious.

Bandages were funny things in those days - plaster of Paris in between knotted lumps of cotton, which set like cement when the perspiration from the hands soaked through. Regular mailed fists! That's how my bandages were that night. What's that, 'Why didn't the other fellow come and have a look at my gloves and complain? He daren't - I might have wanted to have a look at his!"

It wasn't long after this that Gus was topping the bills at South Yorkshire venues and was freely publicised as a champion in the making. Billy Widdowson, a staunch boxing supporter, became Gus' backer and as the good form continued, so did the reputation.

Jim Driscoll, one of the all time greats in British boxing, invited Gus to join his training camp in Cardiff and when Platts defeated former welter champion, Jack Goldswain in 1912, it signalled his arrival in the top flight.

Not long after this, Gus appeared at the National Sporting Club, beating Londoner, Eddie Elton and returned to Sheffield where he beat his main northern contender, Billy Hughes of Hull at Edmund Road Drill Hall.

Over the course of the next ten years or so, Gus Platts took his tally to over 200 fights, including many against the top men in the country and his ability was such that he was beaten less than twenty times.

He embarked on his first trip to America, as many of the top boxers of the day did and distinguished himself in some high class company.

Back home, he had two memorable clashes with another local favourite, Tommy Gummer. Both fights were held at the *Pheasant Inn* Grounds at Carbrook. Gus won the first encounter after being floored several times, and before an audience of 7,000 in the return bout four years later in 1919, Tommy reversed the result, although many of Gus' supporters thought he had at least earned a draw.

In March 1920, Gus met Ted 'Kid' Lewis, the world welterweight champion, but the 'Aldgate Jew' was too good for him and beat him in eighteen rounds. Before they met for a fourth time in a title fight, Gus had two clashes with British Lonsdale Belt holder, Johnny Basham, at welterweight, which ended all square. Basham had lost to Gus in their 1911 fight. Another title contender was Plymouth's Ted Moore who met Gus at the Cosmopolitan Club in Moore's home town. Though really not match fit, Gus took the fight on and despite giving a good account of himself, was beaten on points in fifteen rounds.

As in the fight with Tommy Gummer, Gus' best remembered fights were with local men. There were some good men in South Yorkshire in the years just after the First World War, and to be local champion was nearly as big a feat as being national champion. Gus met the ill-fated Herbert Crossley, who, being much the heavier, was able to beat him. Mexborough's Crossley, brother of future light heavy champion Harry, died in America of pneumonia in his early twenties, in the middle of a career which had yet to realise its full potential.

In the later stages of his career, Gus met Roland Todd at Doncaster's Corn Exchange. Doncaster based Todd, who was on course for a British title and the younger man by ten years was able to win the verdict, although it was close and as with all Gus's opponents Roly certainly knew he had been in a fight!

At the back end of his career in the early 1930s, Gus finally became both British and European champion, although there were problems getting both titles officially recognised. With the bait of a substantial purse, the promoters at the Drill Hall, Edmund Street, Messrs McLoughlin and Cotton, lured Frenchman Ercole Balzac over to England, to meet Gus in his home town. Fought over fifteen rounds, the two men put up a great fight, and the result was one of the best bouts seen in Sheffield for years. After being outboxed in the opening rounds, when he had to rely purely on defence, Gus changed tactics midstream and his constant boxing and mixing tactics had the required effect.

As the contest progressed, Platts took over the fight with his jabs and left leads, worrying Balzac out of it. Immediately there was a challenge for a rematch, this time with his title at stake.

The Frenchman and his manager were keen for a return fight, but because Gus Platts was not British champion (Tommy Gummer was), the European International Boxing Federation's rules would not allow the fight to carry the championship title. If Gus met and beat Gummer, the situation would be resolved, but Platts would have to wait until the Belgian champion, who already had his deposit with the federation, had met Balzac first. Earlier Tommy had travelled to France for the European title, and had been beaten in nine rounds.

A few months later, Gus met Balzac again at the Drill Hall. The controversy whether the fight was for the official title was still in the air but, nevertheless, the bout was arranged under the championship conditions of twenty three-minute rounds. Gus' pal, Jim Driscoll, travelled from Cardiff to witness the fight, and the Drill Hall was packed to suffocation, not an inch of room was wasted in a contest all Sheffield wanted to see. The contest was for £700 and was refereed by Jack Smith.

As in the previous contest, Balzac forced the early pace and his forcefulness made him clear leader after three rounds. Gus came back into the fight scoring well under the champion's guard. When the affair came to a conclusion in the seventh round Balzac was slightly ahead but in evading a rush, the Frenchman slipped through the ropes and apparently hurt his ankle badly. He gamely resumed but the Sheffielder, grasping his opportunity, fought Balzac all around the ring and as the latter could not put his injured foot to the ground, he was compelled to retire, the verdict going to Platts amidst the wildest enthusiasm. It was the highlight of Gus' career, having taken him over 200 fights to win a title, and now Sheffield could boast a European champion and Rotherham a British Lonsdale Belt championship, both at the same weight.

It was later revealed that the International Boxing Union did not recognise the fight as being for the middleweight championship of Europe.

The scene was now set for a third meeting with Tommy Gummer with both titles at stake, although it didn't take place in London. In this period all British title fights were held at the National Sporting Club, under their jurisdiction. Likewise, the Lonsdale Belt, which Tommy Gummer had been awarded by the club, and so the belt couldn't change hands in any contest which Tommy took part in outside the auspices of the National Sporting Club. Not to be outdone, the promoters awarded their own belt to go along with the substantial purse.

This was a fight all Sheffield and Rotherham wanted to see, so why should it be held in London? As both men settled down for strict training at their respective headquarters, Gummer, at the *Flying Dutchman*, Rawmarsh and Platts at the *Red Lion*, Holly Street, the forthcoming fight was the topic on everyone's lips. The event turned out to be a big disappointment for the Rotherham fans, for Gus turned out to be the easy winner.

Soon after Tommy Gummer announced his retirement; a hand injury, which had been plaguing him for some time and which had finally gone during the Platts fight, was the deciding factor. Tommy returned the Lonsdale Belt to boxing's headquarters. Gus claimed the British title and was widely acknowledged as being the holder. After all, he had beaten the British champion, but he was denied the National Sporting Club's official recognition.

Gus' defence of his titles took place only a couple of months after the Gummer contest, when in May 1921 he met Johnny Basham, the Welshman with the most apt name in boxing, at the Royal Albert Hall. Basham had been the first outright winner of a Lonsdale Belt in the welterweight division. Despite being the aggressor throughout, Gus failed to stop Basham piling up the points, the last three rounds tipping the scales in favour of the Welshman.

On realising that his boxing days were coming to a close and that there might not be many more big money matches, Gus decided to take his second trip to America. While in New Jersey he was able to witness the Jack Dempsey versus George Carpentier World Heavyweight Clash in the gigantic arena of 'Boyle's Thirty Acres', in front of the first ever million-dollar gate. He even got an acting part in a film 'The Referee'. Gus' most creditable performance during this trip was against Mike McTigue, the Irish born American. The baseball ground at Dyckman Oval was crowded to see the battle. McTigue closed Gus' eye, but the Yorkshireman was still fighting hard at the end of the fight. McTigue took the decision, but he was a boxer of considerable class, which he proved by winning the world light heavyweight title the following year.

It wasn't long after this that Gus retired. There was the inevitable come-back in 1927, but results were less than encouraging, even though he still had a part to play in Sheffield boxing. He managed several local lads, perhaps the most promising being Don Shortland, one of the last boxers to beat him.

ROLAND TODD

D uring the 1920s when the phrase 'the best defensive boxer in England' was bandied about, it was instantly connected with middleweight champion Roland Todd.

Although he wasn't born in South Yorkshire, he had all his boxing successes in the area and was idolised in Doncaster.

Roland, a Londoner, was born in Marylebone and it was in the capital where he made his first appearance in the ring. Indebted to Andrew Newton for initial training, Roly campaigned quite successfully in the early 1920's as a young middleweight and included among his victories a six round defeat of bandsman Blake, the champion of a year or two earlier.

Moving north because London offered him few opportunities, the partnership between himself and Doncaster promoter and manager Billy Bridgewater, commenced a winning run which would take him to British and European honours and to America to challenge the best in the world.

The career of Billy Bridgewater, a former footballer, had started under the tuition of Alf Greenfield, a former champion of England, but had been curtailed after a fall under a tramcar. Billy had been a promoter around Doncaster for twenty years and his headquarters at the *Black Boy Hotel*, was a hotbed of fistic talent. Billy liked his boxers to live in the area. Jack Kirk, a featherweight from Oldham, moved to nearby Finningley and a popular Irish cruiser, Dave Magill, moved to Doncaster. Billy also had some of the best local men on his books, including popular Doncaster featherweight, Harry Leach.

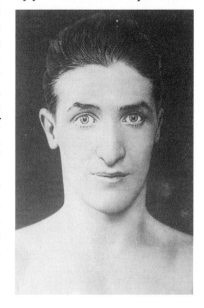

Roland Todd moved to Bentley to begin a very happy association with the area, which continued after his boxing career to his untimely and premature death, while still comparatively young.

From the time he moved to Doncaster, which was around 1920, Roland took part in some fifty contests and wasn't beaten until the time he met Ted Kid Lewis, in November 1922. Never the knock-out specialist, less than half his victories were inside the distance, but his immaculate boxing skill became his instant trademark. A useful left hand and good close quarter work, coupled with his brilliant defensive qualities, made it hard for his opponents to land a punch on him and soon made him a boxer to be much respected.

In Sheffield, Gus Platts had been European champion in 1921. Although now without a title, (his British title was never confirmed by the National Sporting Club), he was still one of the best middleweights in the country and, like Todd, had never been knocked out. A match between the two was a guaranteed crowd puller. Sheffield Sports Association offered £300, for the fight to take place in Platts, home town. W. Parkin weighed in with an offer on behalf of *The Pheasant* at Carbrook, but all Doncaster wanted to see the fight and every effort was made to secure the fight for the Corn Exchange.

Showing all the attributes of a future champion, Todd soon had his supporters on their feet to cheer his scintillating display. The fight went the full distance and in most people's minds there was only one winner, so when referee Jack Smith raised Roland's hand, there were scenes of great jubilation. Platts had a big grin on his face. He'd enjoyed the battle and, taking his defeat like a sportsman, he duly acknowledged his victor.

The next month, May 1922, Roland Todd made an appearance at the National Sporting Club and was most impressive in winning a decisive knockout victory in the twelfth round against Tommy White of Welling. Roland's form in the last twelve months which, besides his Platts victory, had included wins over Jim Watts, Charlie Woodman, Stanley Glen, Eddie Feathers and Pierre Nicholas, put his name forward as a contender for Kid Lewis' title.

What was there to say about Ted Kid Lewis that hadn't been said? One of boxing's immortals, arguably the best British boxer ever, he'd certainly lived up to his nickname 'the dashing, slashing, smashing, bashing, crashing Kid'. Lewis was British and European featherweight champion in 1913, British Empire and European welter champion, which he had held since 1920 (he had also been world welterweight champion on two occasions before 1920) and British Empire and European middleweight champion.

The two boxers had sparred on numerous occasions and Lewis, as

Roland Todd, 'the master of defence'. (*Photo loaned by Bill Matthews*).

usual, never thought much of his opposition.

The champion was touring the London music hall circuit with a revue called 'Hello Sweetie'. The venture had done so well that there were permanent engagements. He had to miss the first house on the day of the title fight, but a notice was displayed outside the Hippodrome at Poplar saying that he would definitely appear in the second house.

Under the auspices of the Sporting Club, the fight took place at Holland Park Hall. The fight went the full distance of twenty rounds. Roland put up a gallant display with his splendid defence being his outstanding feature. The verdict went to the 'Jew Boy', which was booed by some of the crowd, which included over 6,000 of Lewis' Jewish supporters.

Lewis had hoped to end the fight early so he could arrive at the stage door well before the second house was timed to start. Roly's cleverness and brilliant defensive qualities took all the Kid could give, and it was only a sustained rally in the last quarter of the fight that kept Lewis his title. The Kid had all on to make the theatre in time; he did and made a triumphant appearance.

Roland wasn't satisfied with the verdict, he was extremely surprised that he hadn't won, while Lewis stated that he was the most awkward man he had ever met. A return was obvious and there was a lot of interest in the second clash of the boxer versus fighter confrontation. Three months later, the rivals met again at the *Royal Albert Hall*.

Roland was now aged twenty-two and the second fight with Lewis was the highlight of his boxing career. By the sixteenth round it was a certainty that a new champion would be crowned and as the bell ended the twentieth round, Lewis was marked and exhausted. This was Ted's last fight as champion, it was a sore point returning the Lonsdale Belt, as another victory would have made him an outright winner. Some of Lewis' supporters seemed surprised at the result, thinking that Todd had just been a spoiler. The press echoed the result and a film shown later showed Roly received the verdict for his great defence.

Lewis was criticised for being unfit and having spent too much time on the lucrative revue and exhibition circuit. There was only one snag for Roland Todd, because the fight wasn't under the NSC auspices, the Lonsdale Belt couldn't be awarded.

The former champion was still around until 1929 when he retired at thirty-five.

Referee Joe Palmer, who had raised Todd's arm as a middleweight champion of Great Britain, Europe and the British Empire stated 'Todd was a great champion in every sense of the word, his assumed aggression has made a world of difference to his capabilities'.

Collecting £4,000, by far the biggest earnings of his career, the new champion set off home to a 'royal' welcome in Doncaster. They danced in the streets when the result was announced at 11 o'clock at night and they came out in their droves to acknowledge the man they considered their champion. From then on it was a series of exhibitions around the area. Everybody wanted to see the champion in the ring. There was only to be one more fight locally for Roland, before he set sail to America in November.

After a couple of fights had fallen through, Roland, along with Billy Bridgewater and Dave Magill, set sail aboard the *Berensario* for the United States. He had hardly been in America a day, when he met Tommy Loughran at the Philadelphia, New York. Loughran had given Gene Tunney the hardest fight of his career and Tunney would never agree to a return. He had also had a decision over Harry Greb. Loughran took the verdict on points over ten rounds, although the American public booed the result and the press gave Roland equal praise.

Todd's next fight was against one of the hardest opponents he had ever met, Jack Malone from St Paul. Roly lost again but the referee's interpretation of the scoring rules left much to be desired. Bridgewater was convinced Roly could beat Malone and the two men met again and similarly the result appeared unjust. Until he lost the first Malone fight, Todd had been promised a world title fight against the winner of the Greb-Wilson match (Harry Greb beat Johnny Wilson on points, New York, 31 August 1923), but his three losses on the trot put him out of the reckoning. His only victory in America was over coloured fighter, Joey Gans. Afterwards a shin injury put him out of action and curtailed his American sojourn.

On his return home he met Joe Bloomfield and returned to winning ways at the London 'Premierland'. Then it was overseas again and this time to Italy to defend his European title against Italian, Bruno Frattini. Ted Moore whom Roland had already beaten, had beaten the Italian in seven rounds. Frattini had also met Ted "Kid" Lewis and had gone eighteen rounds with the former champion. In front of 20,000 hoarse Italians in Milan, Roland was beaten in his first defence of his European title. Again it was a disputed decision.

In January 1925, Roland met Len Johnson, a coloured man from Manchester, at the King's Hall, Belle Vue. At that time, coloured men were prevented from fighting for British titles and the result was a real surprise. Todd was well below form and although the decision was again close, Johnson won.

During May, Roland travelled to Paris to face François Chantler, who had recently met Todd's conqueror Frattini and recorded a draw. The Paris match was also a draw and once again the decision was disputed. Even the French crowd had thought Todd the victor. During the same month Roland Todd was involved in a most unfortunate accident. Sparring in the gymnasium behind the *Lord Nelson Hotel* in Shambles Street, Barnsley, with Jack Bennett, a 21 year-old Wombwell boxer, the youngster collapsed after six rounds of sparring. The young boxer never recovered and although Todd was completely exonerated from blame, it was a most tragic affair.

Soon after this event Roland Todd and his manager Bridgewater parted company and Roland started to manage his own affairs.

In September 1925 he beat Australian cruiser, Charlie Ring, at Blackfriars. The following month he had a chance to go to Australia, which fell through after Len Johnson, the coloured boxer, beat him in a return match.

After contracting Charlie Harvey, a manager of English boxers in America, Roland made his second Stateside trip. Soon after arriving he was due to meet Maxie Rosenbloom, but couldn't make the weight in time. It was while he was in America and because he hadn't defended his British title, that it was taken away by the British Boxing Board of Control. As on his previous tour Roland's style failed to impress American referees and he quickly lost three matches including one against Harry Greb in Toronto.

On his return to England, there were many other fights for Roland, including a fight billed but not officially recognised for the British middleweight title against Frank Moody, which he lost. It has been stated earlier that Todd had forfeited the title in 1925, when due to his being in America, he wasn't able to defend it.

Todd was never again to reach the heights achieved during his time under Bridgewater but, despite increasing weight, his love of the game was so great that he still made appearances at local 'gaffs' with booth shows like Jimmy Butler's Boxing Show.

Tragically one of his sons died as a young man on the verge of starting his own boxing career and many people believe the tragedy led to Roland's death at his home in Bentley. Many believe he died of a broken heart.

Roland Todd will never be forgotten in Doncaster. They recognised him as their first champion and his name is second only to Bruce Woodcock as their ring hero.

HARRY LEACH

Ted 'Kid' Lewis who was eighteen days short of his nineteenth birthday when he gained the British featherweight title, still holds the record for the youngest British title holder. On two occasions Harry Leach, a younger South Yorkshire boxer, came close to capturing the same record, but Lewis retained it.

Young Harry, who hailed from Woodlands, Doncaster, was only eleven when his boxing career commenced in a spare bedroom at the home of a local trainer. After only six weeks' tuition, he drew with a much older and heavier boy at Mexborough in a £10 a side match. Another contest at 5 stone ringside weight for £25 a side followed and young Harry beat young Lloyd of Wombwell.

As Harry put on weight, contests followed at 5 stone 7lb or 6st with side stakes up to £200. Side wagers in hundreds of pounds accompanied these fights and Harry, who was now billed as the 'Boy Wonder', and still under fourteen was headlining bills in Sheffield, Doncaster and Leeds.

Harry's comments in later life summed up his exploitation. 'I was never consulted and as a boy never received any payment. My only presents were a dressing-gown and a gold medal from two admirers, one an American. Revenue and expenses always balanced with my managers and trainers'.

The youngster's phenomenal rise in the boxing world came to the notice of the National Sporting Club and while still only sixteen, Harry made his debut at the headquarters of British boxing.

Doncaster manager and promoter, Billy Bridgewater, who had guided Roland Todd's road to the top, was established as the leading manager in the area, and had looked after Leach since his early discovery. It was soon seen that working with Todd and lightweight Kirk was good experience for the Woodlands lad.

In April 1924 Harry took part in a series of eliminating matches for the British featherweight title at the National Sporting Club. The title had been vacant since Leeds born Joe Fox had relinquished it during the previous year, freeing himself to tour America.

Harry's opponent in the quarter final was Jimmy Corp of St George's. The fight didn't last all that long. Leach's rifle like right putting Corp down for a series of counts before the knockout punch

arrived. The following month, Harry met Billy Shepherd of Sheffield in the semi-final. Shepherd had qualified by beating Billy Hobbs of Chepstow in his quarter- final match. The London clash of the two South Yorkshire rivals finished in Harry's favour with a fifteen round points win. The youngster arrived back home at Bridgewater's training gymnasium at Balby, having qualified to fight for the British featherweight title. At that time, he was still barely eighteen years old. It is interesting to note that in the 1980s boxers between eighteen and nineteen were limited to contests of no more than twenty-four minutes. The featherweight title fight was fixed for twenty rounds, the first time Harry had fought more than fifteen rounds. In the 1980s the round limit for a championship fight was reduced to twelve.

Harry's opponent in the championship match was George McKenzie from Leith in Scotland. McKenzie had won the ABA bantam title in 1920, but had only recently turned professional.

The fight took place at Holland Park Rink (under National Sporting Club auspices) on 2 June 1924. The money arrangements were a £100 a side and for a club purse of £500. The youngster performed remarkably well and was not in the slightest overawed by the occasion. Leach took the early rounds and rocked the Scot even more with his intelligent left. The odds had been 2-1 on McKenzie but Leach appeared much the nippier. At the end of the fourteen rounds the Doncaster boy was in front on points but it was becoming noticeable that he was starting to tire. The extra five rounds that Harry had before never gone made all the difference. Despite the handicap, Leach hung on grimly to the end. The more experienced McKenzie took control of the fight, particularly in the last two rounds when Harry was out on his feet. The decision was bound to be close. Leach had been in front but had the Scot recovered enough ground to clinch it? To a mixed reception, McKenzie was given the decision. The narrow defeat was a good draw for a return and articles were signed for a re-match six months later.

The following week, Harry was back in London at the Royal Albert Hall, to meet leading featherweight, Billy Palmer. Eastender Palmer was the son of old world bantam champion, Pedlar Palmer, the 'Box o' Tricks'. There were no tricks from young Palmer, he proved himself a very easy victim. The Yorkshireman was never extended and completed a quite easy win, his accuracy and speed being the decisive factors. Staying in London, Harry met Islington's Ernie Swash at the capital's other main venue 'Premierland'. In another one-sided bout Swash, a former amateur champion, was down several times before the referee stopped it to save him from further punishment.

Back home, Harry had spent some of his earnings on a new motor bike and whilst on a joyride he came off and injured himself. Out for several weeks, Harry's luck was still out, when he was summonsed for allowing his brother to use his motorcycle without a licence.

Returning to action at London's 'Premierland', Harry's opponent was Johnny Curley from Lambeth. Curley was a future British featherweight champion, taking the championship from McKenzie in 1925 and losing it in 1927 to another South Yorkshire hero, Johnny Cuthbert. His 1924 clash with Harry Leach was given as a draw. The decision seemed very flattering for Curley and was really a face-saver in front of his own fans.

In the build-up to the return with the champion McKenzie, Harry fought Jimmy O' Donnell of Manchester at the 'Ring', Blackfriars and the occasion almost proved disastrous. O'Donnell delivered what looked like a knockout punch in the first round. Narrowly escaping the count, the bell being the saver, it was only assiduous attention by Bridgewater that enabled Harry to continue at the start of round two. Staying aloof for several rounds while his head cleared, Harry came back to dominate the match and by the fourteenth round O'Donnell's seconds had thrown in the towel to save their man from further punishment.

In November, only a few weeks before the return fight, Harry dropped a decision at the 'Ring'. Harry's opponent was Fred Bullion of Deptford, who had only just lost a very close decision to McKenzie. Harry's tactics were the wrong ones, he made his effort much too late. Even though he won the last two rounds by 'streets', the decision went to Bullion. The winner, much the stronger fighter, had closed Harry's eye quite early in the contest and although the Deptford man won the match, he was criticised in the press as lacking artistry and being too basic.

A month later, at the same venue as their first clash, Harry stepped into the ring with champion George McKenzie in the first defence of McKenzie's featherweight title. Again, the match was scheduled for twenty rounds. Harry had tried to pace himself in the last fight and come strong in the later rounds and had come unstuck. It had been McKenzie who had taken over the latter stages and Harry had struggled to last the distance. The return was fixed at £600 and Harry had still not reached nineteen. The fight followed a similar pattern to the first meeting. Harry gained a promising points advantage and was nothing short of brilliant in the early rounds. His skill won applause from the crowd and his performance left McKenzie with a lot to do to save his title. McKenzie started to come more into the fight from the seventh round. Gradually Harry fell away under persistent pressure from the champion. In the sixteenth and seventeenth rounds, McKenzie was in complete command and, after some fierce exchanges, the challenger seemed lucky to be still on his feet. As in the previous encounter, the youngster tired, leaving McKenzie retaining the championship on a hard-earned points victory.

Though he didn't know it then, the McKenzie return match was the career peak for Harry Leach.

Over the next few years, during which time he fought regularly at Liverpool Stadium, the 'Ring' and 'Premierland', his form was very inconsistent and there were as many defeats as wins. Joe Samuels and Fred Tilston (Chester) beat him at Liverpool and at the 'Ring'. Belgian Desmet knocked him out and Teddy Baker of Bermondsey beat him in a strenuous battle. Harry shared two matches with Charlie Tonner of Rock Ferry. In fact Tonner, in the return match, avenged his previous loss by splitting Leach's nose.

Harry's problem was that even though he was still only nineteen, there were boxers coming into the ranks capable of beating him. Johnny Cuthbert, Sheffield's future champion, earned a draw in their first fight. Cuthbert had gone fifteen rounds, while a young Kid Lewis had a similar result at 'Premierland' on a Sunday afternoon.

By the time Harry was in his early twenties, his career was as good as over. The huge number of fights he had while only a lad had burnt him out.

There was the inevitable comeback, this time as a lightweight and above. The attempt was short-lived; he had his nose fractured by

Harry Crossley, the 12 stone 7lb champion. As Harry stated, 'I was a tiger after the big 'uns and only received my deserts'.

In 1932 there was another comeback for dependants of those killed in the Bentley Colliery disaster. Harry, like many other personalities, fought in many parts of the country for the cause.

Although the demands of boxing made the 'Boy Wonder' a veteran before he reached manhood, Harry Leach, who was very critical of the way he had been treated in later life, along with some of the other stars in Bridgewater's array of talent, helped put Doncaster firmly on the boxing map during the middle 1920s.

Harry himself didn't consider almost winning the British title at eighteen his greatest achievement. He considered that to be in November 1915, when he was aged. He and his brother Joseph, who was two years older, walked twenty-two miles to Pontefract on two slices of jam and bread to see a family friend called to the colours for the First World War.

HERBERT CROSSLEY

In November 1921, the boxing world was shocked to hear of the untimely death of twenty-year-old Herbert Crossley, the Mexborough heavyweight, who had died of pneumonia, while in America.

Although Herbert never became a British champion, he had done enough in his short career to justify his ranking as one of the best heavyweights to come from the north.

Herbert was born in Queen Street, Swinton in May 1901, and was the third of four brothers. His two elder brothers were the first to encourage his boxing talents and they worked tirelessly to further his career. He was interested in physical culture at first and took a correspondence course on the subject. Herbert's first contest was in 1917 when he met a Rotherham youngster at Mexborough's Empire Theatre. His opponent, Quinn, was unable to continue after two rounds and before the year was out, young Crossley had four more victories to his credit. Goldthorpe's Billy Crummack went down at Mexborough, Frank Rylands of Doncaster was beaten on points, and Young Heyland of Wombwell retired after eight rounds and to end the year, Billy Crummack was beaten a second time on points.

The youngster worked, for a while, at Manvers Main Colliery and his fellow miners were keen to see the raw, but eager young boxer make it to the top.

During the month after the fight with Billy Crummack, Herbert had seven fights.

There were wins over 'Luggy' Rodgers, another Mexborough lad, who retired after four rounds, Billy Crummack, who was beaten for a third time, Dick Hepworth of Goldthorpe 'Tosh' Price, of Mexborough and one of the fighting Hague family, George, who he beat on points. Sam Hyde of South Elmsall held him to a draw, while yet another Mexborough boxer, Jack Stanton, became the first man to beat him by winning a points decision, Stanton having much more experience than young Herbert.

As his career began to take off, promoters from further afield began to take notice of him, with Crossley appearing at Sheffield, Doncaster, Manchester and, later, the National Sporting Club in London.

Herbert began 1919 by completing five successive points victories,

A plaque in Queen Street, Mexborough, in honour of the Crossley brothers Herbert and Harry, unveiled by family members. (*Photo loaned by Giles Brearley*).

his victims being Young Cliffe (Sheffield), Charlie Woodhall (York), George Twelvetrees (Worksop), Harold Male (South Elmsall) and Tommy Greaves (Rotherham). The next two matches were drawn. Fighting for the first time over fifteen rounds, Herbert drew with

Seaman Hudson (Worksop), and another South Yorkshire star, Rotherham's Sunny Crofts. Crossley's next appearance was at the National Sporting Club, where he was invited to take part in a novice heavyweight competition. After wins over Sergeant Hilton and Sergeant Thomas in the first two rounds, Herbert qualified to meet Seaman Merrilees in the final. Fight fans had nicknamed the Portsmouth Sailor 'Man Eater', for in an earlier round of the same competition, he had fatally injured Joe Beckett's sparring partner. Maneater or not, Herbert had the beating of the sailor and he was announced the winner. It was especially pleasing for the Mexborough boy, for he was emulating an earlier boxing idol from the same village. 'Iron' Hague had won a similar competition at the Sporting Club in the early 1900s.

As boxers, there was no comparison between the two heavyweights. Hague was a strong man and a hard puncher, while Crossley used a more scientific approach. He was a much more of an athlete than Hague ever was, but he lacked the killer punch, which helped Hague hit the headlines and which took him to the championship. What he lacked in punching power Crossley more than made up for with his ring technique. Speed, stamina, endurance, pluck and ring cleverness were all among his attributes, for there are other ways of winning a fight than by a knockout punch. Throughout his short career, nearly all his wins were on points; very few men failing to go the distance with him.

Herbert's next ring appearance was at Doncaster against Tommy Stokes of Dover. The fight only lasted three rounds and ended in the Mexborough lad being disqualified. It was rashness and inexperience that caused the stoppage, for the wily Stokes was well beaten before he 'oldman'd' the youngster. Will Brooks from Aberavon, a heavyweight well-known throughout the country, was the next boxer to test the aspiring young man from Mexborough. In their first match at fifteen three minute rounds, Crossley took the verdict in an extremely hard fought contest at the Sheffield Drill Hall.

Although the two elder brothers had previously looked after his affairs, Billy Bridgewater became his manager around this time. There was no falling out Bridgewater, the Doncaster manager and promoter, had the necessary contacts to further Herbert's career, but his brothers still looked after his ring business. Also, the quality of Herbert's opponents had risen and Bridgewater's skill and acumen were essential. Windsor's Barney Tooley was soon beaten on points and so too was Harry Curzon.

The Curzon victory was a feather in Herbert's cap as he had

fought for the British Light Heavyweight title a few years earlier.

Herbert returned to London for his next contest against Harry Drake, another leading contender for the lightheavy title (he actually made an unsuccessful bid in 1922). Displaying his best form yet he beat Drake on points.

Herbert's next opponent was Tom Berry, another cruiserweight who was well into his thirties. The fight was a preliminary to the Joe Beckett versus Bombardier Wells, British Heavyweight clash. The ageless Berry was too ripe for the Yorkshire lad and Herbert was beaten over ten rounds in their Holborn Stadium clash. In 1925, Berry won the British Lightheavy title, when he must have been nearly forty. There was always argument about his age and it is very likely he was the oldest boxer to win a British title. Bridgewater was keen for a return and Herbert's next match was against Berry at Manchester's Free Trade Hall.

The fight was marred by Herbert's condition. Arriving in a taxi, he was in a considerably shaken state as he had been seriously delayed getting to the venue and feared he would miss the bout. Although the fight took place as planned, his below par performance only gave him a draw.

Tommy Gummer, the Rotherham favourite, was the next boxer Crossley faced and there was great interest in this local clash. Only a month or two earlier, Gummer had won the British middleweight title, but was not adverse to meeting the lightheavies and heavyweights, having spent his early career fighting them.

The fight took place at Carbrook and in this fight Herbert earned his biggest fight fee in the English ring, namely £147. The clash was a draw in more senses than one. Of the two, most people thought, if anyone, Crossley should have received the verdict.

Tom Berry was invited to have another go at Crossley and the two rivals met for a third time at Doncaster. In his own backyard of South Yorkshire, roared on by his supporters, he was able to beat the vast experience of Tom Berry and square the series with a convincing points win.

Herbert's weight around this time was just above the light heavy limit. Tommy Gummer's main rival for supremacy in the middleweight ranks was Sheffield's Gus Platts.

After the draw with Gummer, it was considered a good match, to put Platts in with Herbert. As so often in the sporting past, there was keen rivalry between Rotherham and Sheffield. In front of Platts' fans in the steel city, the Mexborough teenager (still not twenty) beat the 'Blade Hero' over twenty rounds. To round off 1920, Herbert went to the northeast, where he beat Harry Shoop of London over fifteen rounds at Sunderland.

For his first match of 1921, Herbert was paired with one of boxing's heroes, Harry Reeve. In 1916, Reeve was British light heavyweight champion. When he had come back from the war with a bad leg injury, it looked as if his ring career was over, and indeed he relinquished the title. After a while he made a comeback as a heavyweight and although he never won another title, he was still around for a few years. It proved to be one of the rare occasions when Herbert stopped an opponent, the fight being terminated in the thirteenth round.

In March 1921, Herbert met Frank Ray in Newcastle at St James' Hall. Ray, real name Paul Murray, was a giant 6ft 3in, fifteen stone heavyweight. Ray a year or two back had stopped Tommy Gummer. Crossley suffered a severe setback for the first time since he had lost to Tom Berry at the Olympia. This was also the first time he had not gone the distance in a fight. The referee stopped the fight in favour of the heavier man after seven rounds. Herbert had been down for the first time in a fight and was lucky to survive the knockout. He admitted later that his opponent was too big, saying at the time.

'I realised at once that I must put him out early and nearly succeeded in the third and fourth rounds, but after that I had shot my bolt'.

A few days later, he announced he was concentrating on the heavyweight division. Light heavy weights were keeping away from him therefore he was going to make an effort in the heavier division.

Valuable tuition was gained when, for a while, he became the sparring partner of Australian heavyweight, George Cook, who was campaigning for a crack at the British Empire title. There were only two more fights to come for Herbert Crossley in England, both against heavyweights. In his first, he fought a fifteen round draw with Gordon Simms of Portsmouth and in the second he lost on points to Arthur Townley of Birkenhead.

One of the big disappointments of Herbert's career was that he had never been totally accepted by the establishment at the National Sporting Club. True, he had won the novice competition there, but he had never been invited back. It was the vogue at this time for top British fighters to try their luck in America, so Crossley resolved to make a short trip to the States. Charlie Harvey, the American link man, had seen Herbert fight in London and had urged him to try his luck across the Atlantic. He was reluctant at first, but when Jimmy Wilde offered the same advice, Herbert, on realisation that his English career was at a crossroads, decided to make the trip. Sheffield's Gus Platts had left the country for America and Herbert sailed alone on 20 August 1921, joining Platts' party three days later.

On 26 September, Herbert had his first fight in America when he fought Gene Tunney, the light heavyweight champion of the Expeditionary Force at Dykeman Oval, New York. The fight was scheduled for fifteen rounds, but was cut during the evening by mutual consent to seven rounds because it was getting in the way of the principal event. Incidentally the Gus Platts versus Mike McTigue clash was on the same bill. Gene Tunney was in a different class and although Herbert gave a good account on his American debut, Tunney won the contest comfortably on points. Only a few months later, Tunney won the American Light Heavyweight championship and in 1926, he won the World Heavyweight championship from Jack Dempsey.

When Herbert wrote home in October, he said that two American heavyweights, Jim Coffey and Frank Moran, had been to see him for sparring bouts. Moran had, in fact, seen Herbert fight in England and had been impressed on that occasion. Moran had fought the legendary black boxer, Jack Johnson, for the heavyweight crown in 1914 and gone twenty rounds. There was talk of a fight between Herbert and Coffey, but the latter declined.

In Herbert's last contest he fought Al Roberts and was beaten on points over ten rounds. He lost the decision but won the honours, the referee's verdict being manifestly against the opinion of press and spectators. The Roberts' fight was the beginning of the end.

The same night, Crossley had a temperature and the next day was in bed, with what was thought to be influenza. The illness was, in fact, pneumonia ending in septicemia and Herbert, still only twenty, died in Roosevelt Hospital, New York, a few days later.

The sporting public of Mexborough was shocked that this immensely popular athlete had been so tragically taken when so young and still only in his primary period as a fighter. Only days before his illness, he had agreed to a two year stay in America and now his untimely death had finished what could have been the road to a title fight. The name Crossley did eventually belong to a British champion, when Herbert's younger brother and his greatest fan, won the British Light Heavyweight title, eight years after his brother's death.

HARRY CROSSLEY

There have been many boxing families in the history of the fight game in England, including several champion brothers like the Corbetts, Turpins, Curvis', Finnegan's, and coming more up to date, the Feenans from the north east.

In South Yorkshire, Mexborough produced a pair of brothers in the late 1920s with every right to be in that same quality list, but for tragic circumstances which prevented one of the brothers achieving the necessary champion qualifications.

Herbert Crossley died soon after it was announced he was accepting a two year contract in America. The news of his death from pneumonia was a terrible tragedy for the Crossley family. Though he had never fought for a British title, he had fought several of the contenders and had only been knocked down on a couple of occasions. The news was particularly stunning for Harry. He had idolised his brother and had acted as his sparring partner during training and had been in his corner at most of his fights.

Harry was himself contemplating a career in boxing, but the death of his brother so knocked the stuffing out of him, that it was a couple of years before he started to pick up the threads of his boxing career.

Like his brother, Harry was a miner at Manvers Main Colliery, and some of his workmates helped him to make the decision to go back into the ring. That great Mexborough character of over a decade earlier, 'Iron' Hague, was also an early influence on Harry's career, as he had also been with Herbert.

In 1924 Harry started appearing at local venues and it wasn't long before Billy Bridgewater, the Doncaster promoter and manager, signed him up. Bridgewater, a footballer with Sheffield United and Doncaster in his youth, had already produced one British champion, Roland Todd.

Harry's first victory was over Cyril Devine in Mexborough, while the first man he knocked out was Billy Marsden, a Leeds man, whom he fought at Sheffield.

Knockouts don't figure regularly in Harry's record. Like his brother before him, he never possessed the killer punch to knock men out. What he lacked as a puncher, however, he made up for with his boxing skill. Defence was a strong point in his ring craft, perfectly

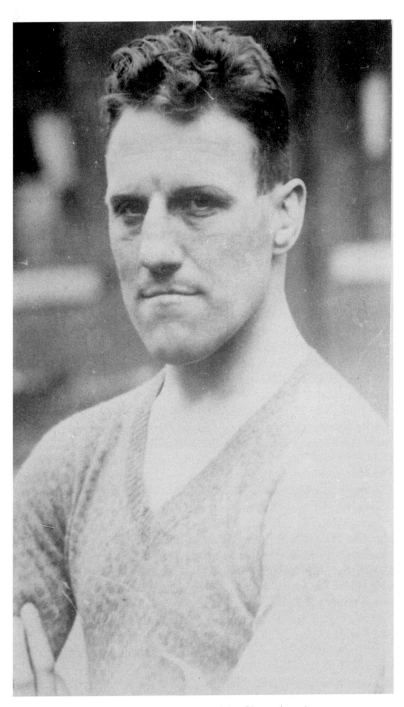

Harry Crossley, British Light-Heavyweight Champion. (*Photo Giles Brearley*).

proved by the fact that he was never stopped inside the distance.

During the next few years, Harry campaigned successfully in the light heavyweight ranks but due to a lack of good opposition, he met men who were considerably heavier. George Slack, one of Doncaster's leading men of the period, was stopped in twelve rounds, while among local victories were wins against Marine Trinder and Stoker Stubbs.

One of Harry's best remembered local fights was his clash with another local lad, Sheffield's Don Shortland. Only eighteen, Shortland outweighed Harry by over two stones, outreached him by two inches and was five inches taller. Gus Platts, who was training Shortland at the Blue Bear, had known the youngster since he was thirteen and had stated in the local press that in his opinion the boy could become a world champion. The fight was labelled as a 'White Hope' contest and top referee, Eugene Corri, was installed as the man in charge.

On this occasion Platts' protege extended his run of victories to eighteen, his machine like left arm being the decider in a points win.

Jack Stanley, the Deptford heavyweight, beat Harry on points, while Len Johnson, the coloured boxer from Manchester, also defeated him on points. Johnson, one of the great boxers who never won a title, also held two decisions over Roland Todd.

There was a trip to Germany where L. Haymann beat Crossley on points.

In June 1929 Harry was matched with Frank Fowler of York for the northern cruiserweight championship. Harry was now reaching the peak of his career and before the Fowler fight had given a superb display in retiring Italian, Primo Ulbaldo, in twelve rounds at Doncaster. Three thousand packed the Leeds National Sporting Club's open-air promotion, to see the two Yorkshiremen fight for the northern title. Harry clearly delighted his supporters with his all-round technically brilliant display, which meant he won every round, bar one. The only disappointment, as far as his followers were concerned, was that despite his decisive victory, he had created glaring openings of which he failed to take advantage. However this was Harry Crossley's way and the kind of sportsman he was. He much preferred a points win rather than knocking his opponent out. To him, boxing was an art and he was a craftsman using his acquired skills, with his hands being the tools of his trade.

Harry's next fight was against former light heavyweight champion, Gipsy Daniels. Gipsy had relinquished the title in 1928 and Bridgewater considered that if Harry could beat the former champion, he would be the logical contender to fight the then champion, Frank Moody. The Corn Exchange at Doncaster was full to capacity and, once again, Harry gave an immaculate display, introducing speed into his attack and using his left hand with great effect. He silenced Mexborough's super critics, who said he was a powder puff fighter. Only Daniels' vast experience saved him from being stopped.

The match with the champion was now on but, before it took place, Harry made another German trip, where he met the Canadian coloured heavyweight, Larry Gains. Larry, who in a year or two would come to England and win the Empire title, beat Harry on points.

The title fight with Frank Moody was fixed for November 1929 at the National Sporting Club. Billy Bridgewater knew all about Moody, as the Welshman had previously defeated his champion, Roland Todd, for the middleweight title. Moody, who had spent considerable time in America, where he met Harry Grebb for the world title, had had difficulty in being accepted by the National Sporting Club as middleweight champion, for his win over Todd was not considered official, as Todd had been stripped of his title for being inactive.

Stepping up to light heavyweight, he had beaten Ted Moore for the vacant title two years previously. It wasn't a sensational fight, few of Harry's fights were, but the result was right and that was what mattered. Harry met everything Moody could give and even found time to bang home his own right. Pacing himself through the distance, the dour Yorkshireman outboxed the champion to take the title on points.

For the second time Mexborough was able to welcome home a British champion. The scenes rivalled 'Iron' Hague's homecoming and the former champion was there himself to pay homage to the new hero when he appeared in a variety show at the Mexborough Hippodrome, where he took part in a three round exhibition match. Coming down the local streets such as Roman Terrace and the High Street, where he was brought up, in his backer James Guest's car was for Harry the highlight of the wonderful reception that Mexborough gave him. He even turned out for Roman Terrace football team in a Mexborough Association match against Conisboro the following day!

During the next couple of years, Harry had about twenty fights and only lost a few. He had a good draw with Len Johnson on his home ground, beat Bridlington's Bob Carvill on points in Newcastle and had two memorable clashes with Reggie Meen of Leicester. Meen, who won the British light heavyweight title in 1931, was beaten in the first match, but squared it in the second fight.

It was May 1932 before anyone was considered to fight for Harry's title. Jack Peterson from Cardiff, a young 21-year-old Welshman, was matched with the 31-year-old champion. Peterson was not long a professional, as only the year previously he had won the ABA light heavyweight title.

The fight was held at Holborn Stadium, where some of the pundits were predicting that Crossley would have too much experience for the youngster. For the first part of the fight, Harry led most of the way and tne points began to pile up in his favour. In the thirteenth round, Peterson managed to catch Harry with his big right hand and he went down. Before the end of the contest, Peterson had dropped him on another two occasions and it was pure guts and resilience that carried Crossley through to the end and saved him from being counted out. The knockdown had swung the points decision the other way and Harry had lost his title. Within two months, Peterson had won the British heavyweight title by beating Rossie Meen and, in doing so, he automatically relinquished the light heavyweight crown.

After the Peterson match, Harry was inactive for a while and then made a small comeback as a heavyweight. Several fights were local, but he then moved to Leicester and ended his career in the Midlands, losing to Germany's Walter Neusal, Jack Peterson and Larry Gains.

Mexborough's sporting public was shocked again, when another Crossley had a premature death. Harry died in 1948, aged only forty-seven.

Harry Crossley will always be remembered as a tactician, sportsman and a gentleman in the ring, who preferred to throw his punches to score points rather than injure his opponent.

JACK KIRK

In 1922 a young lightweight from Oldham came to Doncaster to join Billy Bridgewater's ever growing array of stars. His name was Jack Kirk and along with Roland Todd, Dave Magill and Harry Leach, he helped establish Doncaster as a boxing centre in the mid 1920s.

Residing at Finningley where his father had a farm, Jack Kirk, who was also a Sunday school teacher and a member of the church choir, became one of Doncaster's favourite boxing heroes. In his early days, the youngster could be seen riding on his motorbike over the moors in the evening after work to join in training at Bridgewater's Black Boy Gymnasium.

At the beginning of 1923, Jack Kirk's record stood at forty-two contests with thirty-seven wins and one draw. Though his career had started four years earlier, it wasn't until he became involved with Bridgewater that the lightweight started to bid for honours in his division.

In February 1923, Jack was knocked out for the first time in a bout at Newcastle by a rising young Scots star, Tommy Milligan. It was a poor day all round for Jack, he missed his train from Doncaster and only arrived at the stadium with seconds to spare before his fight. He had been suffering from boils for several days and, to make matters worse, he was given as knocked out by the referee when it looked as though he had beaten the count. The action had only seen two rounds when Milligan had sent Kirk to the floor. When Jack rose from the deck, it was a shock to all that the referee had terminated the fight because he had adjudged Kirk as unable to beat the count. Bridgewater sought a return match and, the two rivals met again the following month at the National Sporting Club. This time Milligan couldn't put him away, although Jack spoilt his chances by concentrating too much on holding and leaning to influence the referee's decision. Milligan completed the double and by 1924 he had moved up to welterweight and won the British title. In the following two years he proved his class by winning the British middleweight title and challenging Mickey Walker for the world title.

In between the two Milligan fights, Jack fought a well-remembered match with another local star, Tommy Gray of Sheffield. There was

Jack Kirk, a leading lightweight during the 1920s. (*Photo loaned by Jack Roake*).

a good deal of interest in this one and Doncaster Corn Exchange was proud to announce a full house for the occasion. Roland Todd was also on the bill in an exhibition match, as were two other Bridgewater fighters, Harry Leach and Sid Smith, who met each other. The Gray-Kirk clash proved as entertaining as any fight seen in the town for a long while.

Gray was a tough and determined adversary and although Jack peppered him with punches nineteen to the dozen, the Sheffielder showed remarkable recuperative powers. The match went the full fifteen rounds with Jack given the result in what was a superb ding-dong struggle.

The Milligan matches had not put Jack's name out of contention for a title fight and, to keep him in contention, he obtained a very pleasing draw with Plymouth's Bob Caldicott who had fought for the title in 1921. Another equally promising result was his win over Welshman, Francis Rossi, who had been on the verge of championship honours for several years.

A match was arranged with Danny Thrush, the Aldgate featherweight, who had only recently returned from America. Sanctioned as a title eliminator the fight had to be cancelled when Thrush was injured.

In May 1923, Hebrew Harry Mason from Leeds had won the lightweight title on a disqualification from Seaman Hall. There was nobody like Mason, 'the man everyone loved to hate'! He was controversial, arrogant, crafty, but most of all he was a crowd puller and fans would travel miles in the hope of seeing someone beat the conceited Jew. Eighteen months before Mason had won the title, Jack had beaten him at the Liverpool Stadium and high up on the champion's list was a return match. There was no doubting, despite his arrogance, that Mason was a brilliant boxer and in the second meeting which took place in Mason's home town at Fenton Street Barracks, Leeds, there was no way Harry was putting up his British and European titles (won at the same time) in a grudge return. Mason pulled out all the stops to take a close decision, but there was trouble at the end when the MC had to remonstrate with one of Mason's seconds. The second, obviously incensed about something, gave the MC a hard blow to the mouth when he had turned to face him.

In January 1924 Jack beat Jim Cater, the former amateur champion of Scotland, at Manchester Free Trade Hall. The match was a most gruelling encounter and there was nothing to choose between either man. Kirk got the decision while the crowd shouted for a draw. The same month Jack travelled to Belfast to obtain a draw with the Irish featherweight champion, Kenny Webb.

Three months later Jack returned to Doncaster with his trainer, Leslie Bridgewater, disgusted over a decision at London's 'Premierland'. Mike Honeyman had been the British featherweight champion in 1921 and was now campaigning as a lightweight.

His match with Kirk resulted in a very surprising draw. It appeared that Kirk had won every round and indeed Honeyman, on several occasions, was very nearly down. In other appearances at the same venue, Jack gave a convincing display to beat Harry Burnstone of Middlesbrough and put a dent in the reputation of knockout specialist Evan Williams from Tylorstown. Williams was completely outpunched by Kirk who hammered him throughout, the biggest surprise being that the sluggish Welshman lasted the distance. Only a day or two before to the Williams fight, Jack had beaten Patsy Coram at Sunderland Stadium.

Harry Mason, the lightweight champion, had been in America in an effort to get a fight with Benny Leonard, the then world champion. Due to his absence, he was unable to defend his title and The National Sporting Club declared it open and a series of eliminating bouts was arranged to decide the new champion.

In the first heat at the Sporting Club in October 1924, Jack gave a brilliant display, beating Birmingham's Arthur Tyrell on points. His convincing style favourably impressed even the partisan London crowd. A fortnight later in the semi-final, Jack was matched against another South Yorkshireman, Harry Robinson of Mexborough. Harry had beaten Bill Handley of Hackney in his heat. The London clash of the two Yorkshiremen proved a great high-speed struggle. Kirk turning it on at the right time to take the decision.

After qualifying for the right to fight for the British championship, it was thought Jack's opponent would be Alf Mancini, the 'KO King' from Notting Hill. Jack had fought Mancini a couple of months earlier at Wembley Stadium. Mancini had taken the decision because he was able to land punches while Jack, for all his brilliant footwork and speed, didn't make enough contact. The other semi-final proved a real shock when Mancini, the red-hot favourite to win the title, was beaten by Ernie Izzard from Herne Hill.

The title fight with Izzard took place at the National Sporting Club in November 1924, for a club purse of £250 and side stakes of £100. Meanwhile Mason had returned from America upset that his title had been taken from him and he duly challenged the winner.

In the match with Izzard, Jack Kirk gave his all in a splendid contest. It was a hard fight; Kirk's speed gave Izzard early problems, but the man from Herne Hill took everything that was thrown at him and came back strongly with counters. Lord Tweedmouth, the referee, cautioned Izzard for using his head in the middle rounds.

In the latter stages of the fight, Jack's left eye bled almost continually, but that didn't stop him from giving his all in the closing rounds. Izzard took the championship, but Kirk took all the applause for a most gallant effort.

Winning ways were soon resumed.

Fred Tilson of Chester was beaten at Chester Stadium, and in the same weekend, Jack was too clever for Phil Walters of Mexborough at Doncaster Corn Exchange, and too experienced for Young Anth of Newport who retired in the thirteenth round at Sunderland. In January 1925 Jack travelled to the Free Trade Hall, Manchester to fight Kid Lees from Oldham. The match was for the Northern Lightweight Championship and belt. Jack was unable to make any impression on the durable Lees who did sufficient to win the title.

Harry Mason the former lightweight champion had, in fact, not been given the chance to retain his title. Instead, The National Sporting Club had matched champion Izzard with Teddy Baker of Bermondsey.

While Harry Mason was waiting his turn with Izzard, he was matched again with Jack at London's 'Premierland'. Jack hated the cocky Mason and rather than miss another crack at the Jew, he took the Sunday afternoon fight despite the fact that he didn't normally fight on Sunday because he was a Sunday school teacher. Kirk put up a splendid display and, although Jack deserved the verdict, the decision was awarded to Mason, amidst howls of protest, the decision being bitterly resented by the onlookers. Kirk had dominated proceedings throughout and even surprised his own supporters with his aggression. It did not seem possible that he could lose, for Mason did nothing but hold.

There were two more fights the same month he beat Dutchman Karel Veld, at 'Premierland' and beat Billy Gilmour, the Irish welterweight champion, at Liverpool Stadium.

In April 1925, the same month Izzard met Baker, Jack took a fight with the Belgian, Lenkamans, at the 'Ring'. Lenkamans had come to England with a formidable reputation and had already beaten the champion Izzard. Kirk gave a brilliant demonstration, completely outclassing the European and giving him a boxing lesson to take home with him. Jack Kirk's next appearance was at Liverpool Stadium, where he made his thirteenth appearance at the famous venue. Thirteen didn't prove unlucky and Jack beat Fred Tilston to complete his thirteenth Liverpool victory in as many visits.

When Jack gave his next London performance, it was against Teddy Baker who had been unsuccessful in his bid for Izzard's title. Jack put himself back in contention by giving Baker a pasting. A few weeks later, in the capital, Jack met Danny Thrush, whom he should have fought a year previously. Thrush, back in good form and himself hoping for a title fight, won the fight on a foul.

In June 1925, Mason beat Izzard to retain his title and before the year was out he had also challenged for the welterweight title, going on to beat Hamilton Johnny Brown, at their second meeting, to regain his second title. Now the title was again vacant, Jack's form deserted him at the wrong time.

In January 1926, at 'Premierland', Sam Steward of Lewisham, surprisingly beat him. In the long run it proved no surprise, for Steward became lightweight champion in 1928 beating the old stager Ernie Rice.

Over the next year or so Jack was still a regular bill topper and a big favourite in London and Liverpool. There were always new lads coming up and Charlie Tanner beat him a couple of times at Liverpool and in April 1927, when he took part in his 100th contest, Bob Miller beat him at the stadium.

Johnny Cuthbert eventually became the first South Yorkshire lad to win the lightweight title when he became champion in 1932.

Finningley based and an adopted Yorkshireman; Kirk had come very near the title and was as popular in his time as any boxer at his weight in England.

BILLY YATES

During the boxing boom of the 1920s and 1930s, the South Yorkshire boxer production line produced a glut of skilful fighters in the smaller weight divisions. Earlier in the period we had seen Walter Fogg of Sheffield, Johnny Lowry of Chesterfield, George Mapplebeck of Doncaster and Sheffield's Tommy Gray. They were soon followed by another good quality bunch, among them Rotherham's Johnny Regan, Swinton's Steve Firman, Sheffield's Dick Inkles, Thurnscoe's bantam challenger Tom Cowley and perhaps the most spectacular of the local flyweights, Billy Yates of Mexborough, known in the early years of his career as 'KO Yates'.

Young Billy had a very similar beginning to another boxing star, Chuck Parker. It was an idle period during the coal strike in 1926, when the very slightly built youngster, then aged sixteen, first donned boxing gloves. Bert Priestley and Sid Breeze had arranged a series of bouts as entertainment for the colliers at the Garden Street Club, Mexborough. When it was discovered they were a boxer short on the programme. Little Billy was persuaded to make an appearance as a last minute substitute and starting off his career on the right track, he received the verdict over Johnny Groves in three rounds. Earning a bob on the side, especially as work wasn't abundant, soon proved popular with the youngster and he started appearing regularly in the weekly boxing shows at Mexborough's *Plant Hotel*. He dropped an early decision to J. Shepherd and was also beaten by Danny Lurches but having followed the two set-backs with two knock-out wins, he was also able to avenge the Lurches' defeat.

On his first appearance outside Mexborough, he went to Leeds and beat Kid Nicholson. Within a year the heavier Nicholson was fighting Kid Pattenden for the British bantam title. The youngster boxed a draw with Ike Simmonds of Sheffield, and went to Manchester where he met Harry Yates of Salford, and beat him on points. Young Billy was gradually building himself up to being quite a forceful little fighter. His numerous minor victories at Mexborough had stood him in good stead and, as he started to appear farther afield, his name was already being noted as one to watch.

Ike Bond, himself a former boxer who could boast a record of over

100 wins, became his advisor, but it wasn't long before former champion Gus Platts took notice of young Billy and, after various try-outs including one in front of Lionel Bettinson, the manager of The National Sporting Club, Billy joined Platts' stable. He received a set-back when a broken bone in his right hand forced him to retire against Sheffield's Billy Hill.

Following a period of inactivity, he resumed where he had left off and, in his first come, back fight, he knocked Hill out. Billy then fought Birmingham's Frank Fowler at Sheffield, but it was a mismatch. He hadn't the experience to beat a man of Fowler's class, and he was beaten on points. There was a third meeting with Hill which was built up as a grudge match, Billy impressing everyone by winning the fight on points.

Yates then made his first appearance in the capital and was beaten by Nipper Daly on points. Daly looked little more than a frail schoolboy, but he was a most brilliant youngster and carried the title 'junior bantam champion of the world'.

Returning home to Yorkshire, the good form continued. Amongst Billy's victims in a lengthy winning sequence were local fighter Johnny Regan, Nottingham's Tommy Kirk and Leeds' Billy Shaw.

By September 1929, the youngster at nineteen could boast a record of forty fights with less than half a dozen defeats and twenty-eight wins by knockout and still no one had knocked him down in the ring. His explosive right hand had earned him the title 'KO Yates', and several opponents and ringside experts were tipping him for future honours. By the end of the year Huddersfield's Stan Butterworth retired against him after taking several counts at the Arcadia (Sheffield), and another London trip had been made. The venue this time was Holborne Stadium, the opponent was Harry Pauling and the National Sporting Club promoted the fight. Billy confounded his followers by adopting strange defensive tactics, and the experience proved costly as he dropped the decision.

His last fight of the year was against another good local man, Steve Firman, of Swinton. Frankie Lane promoted the match as the 8 stone championship of Yorkshire, at Denaby Baths Hall for £20 a side. Firman led from the start and indeed, if the contest had gone the distance, he would have been assured of a points victory. Billy bided his time until the opening came, and when it did in the eighth round, his explosive right hand finished it there and then. Firman was in no state to continue and Billy was awarded the contest on a technical knockout. Firman demanded a return and the parties agreed on a future meting. Billy beat Tommy Kirk for the second time in his next fight at Attercliffe Stadium. The result was controversial and Kirk, who refused to accept the defeat, remonstrated with the referee.

When Dickie Inkles, the Sheffield flyweight, cried off from a fight against Tommy Brown of Salford at Manchester's Free Trade Hall, Billy took his place as a last minute substitute and put up a great fight against a most rough and tough customer. In the first round Billy received a cut lip and, in the fifth, a badly cut eye, while in the eleventh round his other eye was also badly cut, thus ending Billy's challenge in the twelfth round. Billy fumed at the result. He was of the clear opinion that all the injuries, which needed a dozen or so stitches, had been caused by his opponent's head and he was convinced that if the injuries hadn't stopped him, he would have won on points. The Manchester crowd gave him a great ovation and the local press compared him with the great Jimmy Wilde.

On his next trip westwards, Billy delighted the Manchester fans once more with a hard-earned victory over Welshman Cliff Peregrine. Another disputed decision occured when Billy lost to Boy Edge of Smethwick, at Walsall Stadium. Gus Platts was so angry over the home-town decision, that some of the spectators were wondering if, indeed, the former champion was going to make a comeback.

Billy then took part in two fights in two days which gave him as much satisfaction as any others. On the Sunday he beat Wille Sharkey of Newcastle in fifteen rounds at West Bromwich, and laid claim to the Northern flyweight championship. Then on the Easter Monday at Sheffield's Hyde Park, he met Tommy Brown, the man who had cut his face up. This was the match Billy wanted, the last pairing had rightly built the return up as a grudge match. This was also the one the locals wanted to see and they turned up in their droves to watch the local boy make good.

Billy was confident right from the beginning, left leads and right hand hooks figuring strongly in his early performance. Brown was knocked off his pedestal, although he came back in the later stages the damage was done and Billy's revenge was sweet indeed. After the Brown victory, Billy announced he was making boxing a full-time sport and, despite other offers (one came from Fred Dyer's boxing school in London), he was staying with Gus Platts.

During the summer of 1930 manager and promoter Billy Bridgewater started putting on open-air promotions at Denaby United Football Ground. The opening bill topper was the eagerly awaited return bout between Billy and Steve Firman. In a contest fought at a terrific speed, Billy repeated his previous victory over his

Nipper Daly, the boxer with the schoolboy look who beat Billy in his first London appearance. (*Photo loaned by Bill Matthews*).

principal local rival. When the end came, referee Tommy Gummer had no hesitation in holding up Billy's hand.

Appearing at Hyde Park the young flyweight gave two brilliant displays in beating Martin Gallager and Percy Dexter, to confirm his championship potential. At the Dexter fight, an interested observer had been the newly crowned flyweight champion, Bert Kirby. A few weeks later, the pair were matched at Hyde Park in a twelve round non-title bout. Kirby must have seen enough not to put his title on the line.

The contest was made at 8 stone 2lb (2lb above the championship limit). Billy took the fight as seriously as if the title was at stake, going into strict training and using Dick Inkles, and Frankie Depledge as sparring partners. There was a big crowd at the park to see Kirby parade around the ring with his Lonsdale Belt but, not to be overawed, the youngster soon proved he had every right to be in the ring with the champion. Facing his stiffest test so far he came out with a much enhanced performance. Kirby showed that his championship was no fluke, fully demonstrating to the crowd what a clever ring tactician he was. He also proved he had a strong punch, for Billy had the rare experience of picking himself up from the floor and, on one occasion, being saved by the bell. Billy lasted the course but despite his gameness, Kirby was the winner.

George Biddles (less known in the 1930s) was singing the praises of one of his proteges, Tiger Ison. Billy knocked him out, but Biddles was insistent upon a return match. So Billy took him on again and repeated his knockout victory in front of a full house at *The Plant Hotel*.

Later in 1930 Billy took part in the first of several Midlands', engagements. He lost a close decision to Billy James at Leicester, followed up by a creditable draw with Bob Rimmer, a fight he only took on when Rimmer's original opponent, James, was unavailable. His third contest was a classic boxer versus fighter confrontation, against the Welsh champion Jehu, and although he was beaten, there was nothing in it.

Competing as a flyweight in England in the 1930s was very much competing in the top division, exemplified by the fact that for the next twenty years flyweights from Great Britain were to dominate in the world championship at that weight. It was a long hard road to become established and there was no resting on laurels, with many 'up and comers' waiting to step into your place. In other words it was a hard slog to the top, but it was even harder to stay there. This was Billy's position in 1931. Four years of tough campaigning had seen him make the top flight, but a couple of defeats always put him just that step behind.

During the year, two new youngsters appeared on the scene, namely Little Minor of Leeds, and Dick Burke of Liverpool. Minor, in his initial unbeaten run, beat Billy on points while Burke, the first man to beat Minor, destroyed the Yorkshireman in four rounds. Ted Griffin of Bolton also stopped Billy, and the Welsh bantam Terry Morgan forced a draw. There was a well-remembered match with the Egyptian champion, George Aziz, at Hyde Park in front of 12,000 people. Billy, being beaten in twelve rounds, received as much punishment in this fight as he had ever received. However, they weren't all defeats during this poor spell and among several victories was one over Bob Rimmer, with whom he had previously only drawn.

Kirby was no longer British champion; in fact, since he was titleless, he had suffered several defeats, including one by Thurnscoe's Tom Cowley. Billy was matched with the former champion again at Hyde Park in 1932, but the lad from Mexborough only showed flashes of his old form, the bout terminating in the eleventh round when Yates was disqualified for holding.

There were to be other fights for Billy, but the fire had gone and his best years were over. Out of all the fistic talent that came out of Mexborough, Billy Yates attracted special affection among boxing fans as the little 'KO king', a giant of the small division.

Both the author and the publishers have engaged in considerable researches in their attempts to locate an illustration of Billy Yates, including liaising with numerous collectors and dealers in boxing memorabilia and sporting historians. The publishers have made appeals on local radio and the author has written numerous letters to contacts in both the world of boxing and among his many friends in the sporting press. Sadly neither pictures, or programmes featuring Billy Yates have come to light anywhere. We apologise for this omission.

JOHNNY CUTHBERT

Johnny Cuthbert was the first officially recognised champion from Sheffield to hold British titles at two different weights. Although he was sometimes criticised for being a light hitter and using the open glove, he was exceptionally fast on his feet. So clever was he in defence, that boxers found it difficult to catch him with a good punch, a valuable attribute for a champion who kept Sheffield in the boxing limelight throughout the late 1920s and early 1930s.

Born in Darnell in 1904, Johnny, commenced his boxing career at St George's Church School, where the Revd. Harold Ewbank put him through his early paces. Convinced he was going to make headway in the fight game, he turned proffessional at seventeen, wisely making his father Jack, who was landlord of *The Brown Cow Inn* in Sheffield, his manager.

Training at Harvey Flood's gym in Fitzwilliam Street, with Ben Stanton as his trainer, Johnny, began appearing at many of Sheffield's, professional venues in the early 1920s. He won his first fight by knocking out Horace Millward at Somme Barracks, and soon came to the notice of promoters Gus Platts and Fred Ketton, who helped launch him on his early career. Johnny was a bantam in those days and after only some half dozen fights he met Harry Leach, another South Yorkshire youngster who was chasing honours. In his first fifteen rounder Johnny held Leach to a creditable draw. A few more fights and Johnny earned the right to fight the British champion, Johnny Brown, by beating Fred Hindley in a title eliminator. However, Brown was in America, and on a suggestion from Fred Hindley's manager, Sam Hurst, Johnny followed suit. Sports writer Norman Hurst travelled to America on a booked ticket with Johnny accompanying him as a stowaway. Johnny had difficulty in getting fights and the two he did have were both as a last minute substitute and were both lost on points. This made the trip a frustrating experience and he returned home slightly disillusioned and considerably overweight. On such occasions, his father Jack used to seal a room at the pub, locking all the doors and windows, creating a hot room heated with a coke stove in order to sweat off the excess pounds.

Back in training and picking up the threads of his career, Johnny

Johnny Cuthbert, British Featherweight Champion 1927-28, 1929-31 and British Lightweight Champion 1932-34. (*Photo loaned by Bill Matthews*).

soon got back to winning ways.

Boxing now as a featherweight, the Sheffielder made his debut at the National Sporting Club, meeting Harry Corbett, a rated fighter from the East End. His London appearance was a success, for he beat Corbett, on points. His battles with Corbett later in his career when championships were at stake would produce pure boxing classics.

Johnny's progress was so rapid that by January 1927, he was matched with the British featherweight champion, Johnny Curley, at the National Sporting Club. Curley had been champion since 1925 and had met every featherweight of note, and top lightweights too. He had put two exceptional unbeaten runs together (twenty-seven fights in 1920 to 1922 and 29 fights in 1923 to 1924) and had won the Lonsdale belt outright. Although the fight was very close, Johnny emerged victorious and almost everyone in Sheffield turned out to see their hero return home. Johnny turned out to be Curley's bogeyman; the pair met four times and Johnny would win all four on points. No wonder later Curley would claim, 'it was like fighting a ghost'.

Only a week after his title triumph, Johnny topped the bill at Edmund Road Drill Hall against Belgian, François Sybille, who during his career won the European title four times. The title fight had gone twenty rounds and the clash with Sybille went fifteen. No way was Johnny going to lose after the reception his home fans had given him and he finished strongly to win his second fight in successive weeks. Harry Corbett, who had already become Johnny's greatest rival, was given another chance to win the featherweight title a year later. He had originally made an attempt to beat Curley when he was champion but had been unsuccessful. This was the sixth meeting between the pair, with Cuthbert having already won three and drawn one. The two rivals met eight times in all with Cuthbert winning four and two being drawn, all the fights going the distance 118 rounds in total. Johnny and Corbett's twenty round match took place at the National Sporting Club in March 1928 and Corbett came home without his title.

Previous to the title loss, Johnny had made several visits to Paris to take on some of the leading European boxers. In January 1928, after beating Gustave Humery and Edourad Macart on earlier visits, he met Andre Routis. The fight was a classic and the result was a popular draw. Later in the year, Routis won the world featherweight title from Tony Canzoneri, at Madison Square Garden, New York.

A year after the Corbett defeat the two rivals were matched again for the title in 1929. The fight became a landmark for two reasons, it was the first British title fight over fifteen rounds (the Board had moved it from twenty), and it was the first title fight to result in a draw. Referee Douglas' decision gave a good reason for a quick re-match and Johnny and Corbett met again for the Londoner's title.

The occasion, only two months later in May, was another landmark for British boxing, for it was the first time that three British title fights were contested on the same bill. In a National Sporting Club promotion at London's Olympia, Len Harvey knocked out Alex Ireland for the middleweight title in an all time classic, Teddy Baldock outpointed Kid Pattenden for the bantam weight crown and in their seventh meeting, Johnny Cuthbert regained his British featherweight title from Dick Corbett. It seemed as if a draw would again be the verdict, but, to the surprise of some, Johnny was given the decision.

Johnny fought regularly at Liverpool Stadium during this period and soon became the favourite of an acknowledged boxing audience. Performing at Liverpool at the same time was another champion in the making, local lad Nel Tarleton, and it was inevitable that the two would eventually meet in the championship ring.

Meanwhile Johnny had another title defence to make and by beating Liverpool Italian Dom Valente, the stylish Yorkshireman became the outright winner of a Lonsdale Belt. The talk of the fight with Nel Tarleton resumed with Liverpool Stadium proposed as the obvious venue. Previously every recognised title fight had taken place in London but, on this occasion, the National Sporting Club gave permission for the fight to be held in Liverpool.

The fight took place on 30 November 1930 and although the crowd was with Nel, the referee couldn't separate them and Johnny was still champion. The draw was a certain money-spinner for a rematch which was again fixed for Merseyside later in 1931. During the year Johnny had been taking several fights as a lightweight (his rival Corbett had also moved up the ranks). It was known that Cuthbert had weight problems and stories circulated about him having nothing to eat for 48 hours before a fight and, when he was in London, he was known to spend the night before a contest in a Turkish bath.

Only a month after the Tarleton draw, Johnny fought the lightweight champion, Al Foreman. The champion had spent most of his career in Canada, only returning recently and winning the title at the first attempt at 'Premierland', in May 1930.

Cuthbert made a very valiant bid to end the year as a double champion. The clash ended in another title draw and the third such encounter in which Johnny had taken part in. He received £650 for the title fight, his highest ever earnings. His first title fight against

Curley had only brought in £150. Later in life, he was very cynical about latter day fighters who had quicker opportunities to land a big purse and not having to battle through scores of fights to get one either.

A popular visitor to the British shores in the early 1930s was the 6ft negro, 'Panama Al Brown'. Brown was the world bantam champion and obviously to weigh 8 stone 6lb, and be six feet tall, he was a ring 'freak'. Brown was on a barnstorming tour of Britain, beating the best of our featherweight and bantamweight fighters. On his inaugural British tour, Johnny was the only man to beat him and that was on a disqualification.

In October 1931 came the return bout with Nel Tarleton. Liverpool was again the venue and Cuthbert lost his featherweight title for the second time when the local man beat him on points. This was Cuthbert's last effort as a featherweight. Difficulty making the weight made him decide his future was as a lightweight. For Nel Tarleton there were several more championships. Over the next ten years he regained the title twice and retired in 1947, aged forty-one, as undefeated champion.

Now in the higher division, Johnny started 1932 with a couple of wins over Barnsley's Chuck Parker, and another victory over Dom Valante, which the Boxing Board sanctioned as an eliminator for Foreman's title. The run was spoiled by a defeat at the hands of the European Champion, Cleto Locatelli of Italy. Pressing for another chance at Al Foreman, the lightweight champion, his claims became thwarted when Foreman refused to agree on the purse. After Foreman had departed for Australia, the Board deprived the champion of the title and Johnny was named to fight Scot, Jim Hunter, in a decider at Glasgow in August 1932. The Scottish champion, Hunter, was very much the favourite, especially as he was fighting in his own backyard. Johnny knew that to come away victorious from a seething crowd of 'Jocks', baying for an Englishman's blood, he would have to knock out Hunter to get a result and that is precisely what the Sheffield lad did. In the eighth round, the Scots were quelled to silence when their champion hit the canvas. By the tenth he had taken two more counts and received the final knockout blow. Johnny had won his second British title and his first inside the distance. What a hero's welcome he received, the Sheffield people gave their new champion a rapturous welcome!

During 1933 his Sheffield fans were able to see their own champion in action at Hyde Park. Disastrously, he dropped a decision on his home-town appearance against François Machtens, but he was able to avenge it a few weeks later when he beat the Belgian in a return match.

Johnny's form did start to suffer during 1933, and it was obvious that his career in the top flight wasn't going to last too many years more. During January 1934 he was called upon to defend his title against the 'Ice Berg Jew', Harry Mizler. Harry, a brilliant amateur, had been three times ABA champion and had won the gold medal at the Empire Games in Canada. He was nine years younger than Johnny and was very much the man in form, having won over a dozen fights in an unbeaten run to clinch a title fight.

The clash took place at the Royal Albert Hall and, as expected, Mizler won the title but not before Johnny Cuthbert had given him the fight of his life. The London audience was so appreciative of the former champion's vain attempt that they gave him a standing ovation and clapped him all the way to the dressing-room. After the Mizler fight Johnny was ready to call it a day.

Johnny Best, the Liverpool promoter, knowing how popular Cuthbert was on Merseyside, asked him to fight Seaman Watson. Watson had beaten Tarleton for the featherweight title and Best was hoping Johnny would come back and regain it. A serious match was out of the question. It was too much to ask to drop back down a weight, so the match took place at catchweight. Watson won the contest but only by the narrowest of margins. World champion featherweight titleholder Freddie Miller, from America, was currently in England. Nel Tarleton, who had beaten Watson to regain his British title had been outpointed by the champion so to restore some pride, Johnny Best persuaded Cuthbert, who had already announced his retirement from the ring, to make yet another appearance.

Fighting at catchweight, Johnny was well beaten and the result signalled the end of his illustrious career.

After retiring, Johnny took a pub at Boston, Lincolnshire and resided there afterwards. Very hard of hearing in later life, he was still active enough to be a member of the Sheffield & District Ex-Boxers' Association.

In his time he was one of the country's greatest boxers and he never forgot his early background in the Sheffield streets. In later years one of his greatest pleasures was to be able to take groups of poor children from the area where he had begun his boxing career, charter a charabanc and take them off to the seaside, many of them for the first time.

CHUCK PARKER

Barnsley had the distinction of producing one British champion when Charlie Hardcastle won the featherweight title during the First World War. During the 1930s the coalmining town came near to proclaiming a second, when the area's own Chuck Parker, who was only six when Hardcastle put Barnsley on the boxing map, challenged for the welterweight title.

Nicknamed Chuck because there were already two Charlie's in the Parker household, young Parker first donned the boxing gloves during the idle periods at his job in the mining industry. Encouraged by his displays with his workmates, the next stage was to commence gymnasium work at Fred Holden's gym off Sheffield Road. Holden's gym, which was later run by Bill Birch, was the training centre for Barnsley's foremost ring exponents. Billy Jones, Jim Birch, Jack Skelly, that good bantam from Cudworth, Bob Watson and the likeable Matt Moran were all regulars, and even Hardcastle himself, though retired, popped in to give advice. Nine months after his first gym work Chuck, at sixteen, made his debut in the Drill Hall at Barnsley. Only days before his first fight, Chuck had hurt his right hand, but nothing was going to stop him from appearing in the ring and although the injury was the main reason for his defeat, Chuck wasn't dispirited. His handicap had made him use his left hand more and was good experience for the apprentice boxer.

A week later at the same venue Parker gained revenge by out pointing the same opponent, Frank Marshall.

In his next half a dozen fights, young Parker suffered only one defeat and by his eighth fight he was appearing at the top of the bill. Chuck defeated Curly Williams at Normanton, and in his first ten round match fought as a substitute for Billy Jones against Manchester's Jack Hudson. Several appearances were made at Preston, where Chuck became popular and when the Preston promoter held a belt competition for lightweights, at which weight Chuck was appearing regularly, the Barnsley youngster was invited to enter. Chuck had the misfortune to draw Jim Learoyd of Leeds, the Northern Area champion and a veteran of many ring wins. The experience of Learoyd proved too much for the youngster and the victor showed his prowess by winning the final.

Chuck Parker, Barnsley's popular welterweight of the 1930s.

In the same Barnsley back streets as Chuck, lived Billy Jones - Barnsley's Northern Area lightweight champion. Jones, the older by five years, had earned the honour of being the town's top boxer and Chuck's rapid rise over the last few months had started to threaten his position. Deadly rivals in the late 1920s and early 1930s and good friends in later life, it was only natural the two men should meet in the ring. The meeting was at Dearne Football Club one Monday. Jones proved too clever and carried too much experience for the youngster and gained a victory.

Following the experience of twenty or thirty more victorious fights and desperately keen for a return, Chuck made another challenge to Jones. Chuck was still managing his own affairs and would have fought for nothing to have the chance of beating his rival. The rivalry had made the fight a grudge match and so keen were fight fans that Barnsley Stadium (where the town centre bus station now stands) was packed. The fight captured Barnsley's imagination and money changed hands like nobody's business as the townsfolk betted on their individual hero. Unfortunately, the affair, much to the huge disappointment of the fans, only went on for one round. Chuck was disqualified at the end of the first round for allegedly hitting after the bell.

Chuck's next big fight was against another local hero, Sheffield's former featherweight and soon to be crowned lightweight champion, Johnny Cuthbert. Made as a catchweight and jointly promoted by Walt Hattersley and Sam Usher at the Imperial Hall, the match created so much interest that the overspill from the Imperial resulted in promotion on the same night at the nearby Stadium. For the first nine rounds Chuck exceeded all expectations and gave a brilliant display. It was thought in some circles that he might be overawed at meeting a man of Cuthbert's class, but with Chuck the better the man the better he fought and the best way to learn was to fight the best. In the tenth Cuthbert put him down and for a round and a half Chuck was oblivious to what was happening. It was only when his close friend and trainer Harold Huxley had sponged him with water, that he came back in the twelfth round to finish second in a great fight. A return match was arranged to be staged at Edmund Road Drill Hall, Sheffield, but this time the weight was stipulated at 9 stone 6lb. Chuck had to lose weight and obviously that had some bearing on the result, although there was no way that Chuck wanted to use that as an excuse. Cuthbert wasn't far short of world class and consequently he repeated his first victory. Johnny was so impressed by the Barnsley boy that he invited him to become his sparring partner. From then on the two fighters became firm friends.

During 1932 he met Cuthbert's great rival Harry Corbett, the former featherweight champion. In front of his own crowd Corbett won the decision, but Chuck was learning all the time and his next fight was a victory over Jim Learoyd. During the year he beat Vic Maudsley of Preston, Jack Lord of Bolton, Leo Phillips, Carl Barton and Don Jones, the Welsh lightweight champion whom he knocked out in four rounds.

Chuck's form continued to improve and boxing regularly in the Midlands, he knocked out Peter Nolan of Walsall, beat one of the famous Moody family, Jack the Welsh welterweight in nine rounds and had a points victory over Freddie Dyer of Smethwick.

Journeys were made to Scotland and he drew with Willie Hamilton at Parkhead open air stadium, before returning to beat Hamilton on points on a subsequent occasion. Another eight matches without defeat were followed by a draw with Pat Haley. Len Wickwar was overcome at Barnsley, Willie Hamilton was defeated at Edinburgh in four rounds and Chuck travelled to Brighton, where he took part in a very debatable draw with Fred Webster, the former lightweight champion. Pat Butler from Leicester, later to become welterweight champion, was defeated at Barnsley and that victory was followed by another ten straight wins.

Chuck Parker was now on the verge of a title fight. He had been boxing predominantly in the welterweight division and his successful run of form had made him a contender for the title. A set-back was received at the hands of another contender, Dave McCleave, who beat Parker on points in London. Chuck bounced back in the best possible way by beating Canadian Paul Schaffer. The tall colonist was taking all before him in the welterweight division and Chuck's victory was Schaffer's only defeat in his first sixteen matches. Chuck achieved victories over Stoker Reynolds, who had been a title contender, Jack (Kid) McCabe, Jack Daley from Wigan, who lasted three rounds and Kid Kelso. The return with Schaffer was Chuck's next fight and after another creditable display he was matched with the South African, Panther Purchase. Over the space of the next few months he beat Purchase twice, the second fight being at Sheffield. It looked as though Chuck was going to achieve a victory over the wily double champion, Harry Mason, when a cut eye altered his progress in the ninth round.

Chuck's next honour was to become Northern Area Champion, when he forced Pat Haley to retire in the fourth round. The bout was sanctioned as an eliminator for the welterweight title. Chuck's next opponent was another leading challenger Ginger Sadd who was beaten on points at Norwich. Chuck then fought a classic draw with seaman Jim Lawlor, whose great performance against Canadian, Sonny Jones, had seen the 'Ring' magazine rate him number eight in the world. In the return match at Belfast, Lawlor proved the better man and was awarded a points victory.

In the lead-up to what was to become a title fight, Chuck drew with Canadian Tommy Bland, the man who had broken Cuthbert's jaw, beat Mansfield's Mick Miller in five rounds and lost on a cut eye to Belgian champion Lewis Seereans at Leeds. In the next round of the title elimination, Chuck's opponent Charlie Baxter withdrew with illness leaving Parker with a bye to the final.

Ernie Roderick had beaten Dave McCleave in the other match, leaving the Liverpool man to fight Chuck for the title which had become vacant on Pat Butler's retirement. Before the fight at Liverpool in 1936 could take place, Roderick was suspended for six months for a breach of Boxing Board rules, so Dave McCleave whom Roderick had beaten was matched with Chuck for the title in the following month.

The fight was held at Earls Court on 15 April 1936. London meat market porter McCleave was a three times ABA champion and in 1932 had represented Britain in the Olympic Games at Los Angeles, where he bowed out in the quarter-finals on a close verdict to the eventual Olympic champion. The fight was on the same bill as another championship fight, a heavyweight clash between Jack Peterson and Jock McAvoy. The welterweight clash was considered very much a secondary affair, the main attraction being the battle of the heavyweights, although McAvoy was only just over middleweight. As events turned out, the Parker versus McCleave contest was the face-saver. The big fight proving so dull that the crowds were giving the slow handclap. Chuck Parker gave all he had. It had taken him about 150 fights to get in the championship ring and one thing for sure, the pride of Barnsley was going to make McCleave know he had been in a fight.

There was no doubting McCleave's class. On the night he was the better man, but he needed all his skill to withstand Chuck's attack. Chuck took a lot of punishment in his valiant attempt and, despite a great effort in the last round, when he did everything possible to snatch a last minute victory, the title went to McCleave.

A warm reception from his friends in Barnsley was little compensation and instead of his weekly fight which had been his form since his career had started, Chuck took a thirteen week rest.

During that period of rest McCleave had lost his title to Jake Kilrain in Scotland, after only being champion for six weeks. When Chuck felt ready once more to resume his ring career, his comeback match was against the champion in a non-title bout. Kilrain's name was, in fact, Harry Owens, but when he took up boxing, he decided to call himself after the famous old bare-knuckle prizefighter. The comeback proved unsuccessful, for the new champion beat Chuck on points.

Chuck's career lasted another eighteen fights. Although there were one or two defeats including one against Jack Lord of Bolton, for the Northern Area title (Lord was, in fact, the next challenger for Kilrain's welterweight title), he was forced to retire after an operation for a detached retina resulted in him losing an eye. It was heartbreaking for Chuck to give up the sport he loved after a career of 170 fights, plus many unrecorded bouts in boxing booths. His career came to an end at the age of twenty-seven.

After the war Chuck still kept an interest in boxing, running several boxing gyms, including at his places of employment, Fox's Steelworks at Stockbridge and Slazenger's at Mexborough Dyke.

Chuck retired to Barnsley, the town he never left and where he deservedly holds a place as one of Barnsley's best loved sons.

PART TWO
SECOND WORLD WAR TO THE PRESENT

HENRY HALL

After a few years in the doldrums, and just when boxing in Sheffield was starting to take off again, the steel city was rocked in 1979 by the premature death of the popular Henry Hall. A man who won the respect of his fellow professionals, a man good enough in his time to be British welterweight champion, Henry gave his life to boxing in Sheffield, the tragedy being that, when Brendan Ingle was deservedly receiving accolades for putting Sheffield boxing back on the map, Henry Hall, who had done so much in local circles, was not there to be a part of it.

Henry began his career as an amateur with the Hillsborough Boys' Club, and maintained his connection with the club up to his death. Even after a hip operation in 1976 he remained reluctant to give up his job as coach. Boxing wasn't the only sport he was interested in as a youngster. He was a member of winning teams as a cross-country runner, a fair table tennis player and a good average footballer.

By the time he was sixteen, Henry had already won the Northern Counties junior welterweight title. He progressed to the senior title at eighteen and by the time Henry was nineteen he was boxing in the ABAs. In 1944 Henry Hall realised his first dream by becoming ABA champion.

In January the following year, Henry turned professional leaving behind an amateur record of 135 fights with only nine defeats, his successes including two victories over Johnny Ryan. Fellow Yorkshireman Bruce Woodcock introduced Henry to his manager Tom Hurst, and thus began a happy association which would eventually lead to Henry's title victory. Bruce and Henry became firm friends and when they were on the same bill, the first thing they would do was to look for the other's result.

After winning his first half a dozen fights, Henry was matched with Eric Boon, one of boxing's greats. Boon, lightweight champion from 1938 to 1944 (the legendary manager and promoter Jack Solomons had made his name through Boon's wartime exploits in the ring),

Henry Hall, of Sheffield. British Welterweight Champion 1948-49. (*Photo loaned by Bill Matthews*).

had taken part at the beginning of the war in one of the most classic matches ever to have taken place in this country. Even today, Boon's thrilling clash with Arthur Danahar, is well remembered as an epic of boxing history and always near the top when polls of the greatest fights are taken. Boon had experienced weight problems and since losing his title had moved up to welterweight. The night was a double celebration. Bruce Woodcock won the heavyweight title from Jack London (father of later champion Brian), and Henry had his best win to date, knocking out the much more experienced ex-champion in four rounds.

Henry's continuous run extended to thirteen victories before he lost on points to Ginger Stewart at Manchester.

Hall started the 1948 season with his name linked to a possible challenge for the British title. There were several other men in the same bracket and Henry had to go through eliminating matches to earn the right to meet Ernie Roderick. Ernie had been champion for nine years and the title was regarded as Liverpool's private property. The season didn't start too successfully for Henry. He went to Belfast and was outpointed by Tommy Armour over eight rounds. On his return to Sheffield the following month, he showed his class by beating a European boxer, Joseph Goreux of Belgium. His clear-cut victory at Edmund Road Drill Hall saw him matched with another title aspirant, Scottish champion, Willie Whyte. Another devastating display in front of his home crowd, when his sheer skill and workmanship overwhelmed the Scot, brought Henry's name forward as the leading challenger.

Tommy Armour, Henry's victor earlier in the year, was named along with the Sheffield man to fight in an eliminator, the winner to fight Roderick. It was hoped to hold the eliminator in Sheffield and the date was set for July at Edmund Road Hall. Then the venue had to be changed when it was announced that the hall was unavailable. Not to be outdone, promoter Walter Hattersley and matchmaker Jack Greaves, keen for the fight to be staged in Sheffield, took the risk of booking Sheffield Wednesday's ground at Hillsborough for an open-air promotion. It had been a long time since open-air boxing had been held in Sheffield, but Henry was especially pleased to be able to fight there. Hillsborough was his own backyard and he had a special affinity with the football club. He had played for them in goal and as centre forward during the war and did most of his training there.

For the first boxing tournament ever held at the football ground, a crowd of 13,500 turned out to see the local hero's campaign for a title shot. Henry had a new dressing-gown especially made for the occasion. The gown, in Sheffield Wednesday blue, carried the owl mascot and no one could have been prouder as he entered the ring. It took time to adjust to Armour's southpaw style, but gradually Henry took over and the points started to add up. Taking the accolade from the Owls' fans, Hall's points victory set out the score for a clash with Roderick.

There were hopes of holding the fight at Hillsborough, but Roderick's injured arm prolonged arrangements and the fight took place at Harringay in November 1948. Roderick was the clear favourite and he was so confident of winning that he didn't even bring his Lonsdale Belt with him. Roderick was mistaken and Henry caused a major upset when he took the title, although the decision was hotly disputed. Henry had never gone fifteen rounds before and Roderick's plan had been to contain him early in the fight and take over in the latter stages. In the 'War of the Roses', Roderick definitely won the last four or five rounds but Henry had done enough to be called champion by his work in the early and mid-fight rounds to clinch matters. Henry's sporting gesture of running over to pat Roderick on the back before the referee had announced the result, gave the notion to many in the crowd that Henry was acknowledging Roderick as victor. But this was the type of sportsman Henry was and a typical gesture from the man. When the decision was announced pandemonium broke out. The booing was loud and long and two bouts later arguments were still going on.

Henry's next appearance was as champion at Edmund Road Drill Hall fighting the Belgian, Willie Wimms. The affair finished disappointingly in the fifth round when the Belgian retired with rib injuries.

In February 1949 Henry was booked for Harringay again. After his last appearance when he had been booed out of the ring, Henry was determined it wouldn't happen again and this time he received the cheers by beating American, Tony Janiro. Despite being badly cut, Henry gained the best victory of his career in this fight. The American, only in his twenties, launched some roughhouse attacks, but despite some doubtful tactics by Janiro, Henry was a clear winner. Twelve months later Janiro drew with Rocky Graziano.

In July, on the same bill as the Woodcock versus Mills fight at the White City, Henry had his first chance to get into the European ratings. Frenchman Titi Clavel, a challenger for the European title, looked as if he was finished after four rounds. Henry had cut him in the first round and in the fourth referee Teddy Waltham all but stopped it after examining Clavel's eye. However, in the fifth, the Frenchman cut loose and Henry was down three times before Waltham stopped it.

The defeat was one of three Henry suffered in the few months before his next title fight was fixed, not exactly the best preparation for his title defence. The next challenger was Eddie Thomas, the singing Welshman from Merthyr Tydfil. Thomas, who was to earn later fame as manager of world champions Howard Winstone and Ken Buchanan, had met Henry only nine months before the championship title win. The challenger had beaten Hall on that occasion and to further his challenge for the title, Thomas had beaten the elder statesman Roderick in a title eliminator.

The two were matched at Harringay in November 1949, almost a year to the day after Henry had won the controversial decision over Roderick in the same arena. Thomas' spoiling tactics paid off and the fight was badly marred by the referee's handling which allowed too much holding. Henry had entered the ring with a black eye earned in training and by the ninth round his nose was bleeding so much it affected his breathing. Excitement came in the thirteenth round, when Henry fell to the floor in obvious agony. Thomas' punch was on the verge of being illegal and it is debatable whether the Welshman would have been disqualified if Henry had been unable to continue. As it was, the game champion was up at nine wanting to continue and Thomas escaped with a severe caution. The knockout proved to be the deciding factor in the fight, for Thomas was able to turn on the pressure in the last two rounds. Thomas' final fling especially in the last round, tipped the scales in his favour. There was no complaint from Henry, he duly acknowledged the better man had won.

After this defeat, Henry became a middleweight. He even changed managers coming under Nat Seller's wing.

It became a struggle to find consistent form; although there were still several victories, top men like Alex Buxton (light heavyweight title winner 1953) and Johnny Sullivan (middleweight title holder 1954) beat him.

Never again achieving the heights as he did in the welters, a couple of years later Henry retired from the ring. His last fight being a loss on points to Sammy Milsom, at Bristol.

Like many retired fighters, Henry's love of the game was too great for him to absent himself completely from the world of boxing. The ex-champion became a referee (he was also a football referee in the Sheffield leagues), and he still took a big interest in the boys' clubs where his own career had started. From his boxing earnings Henry bought a dairy and became Sheffield's most popular milkman.

His great interest in the sport led him to become a founder member of the Sheffield Ex-Boxers Association. At the time of his death he was president of the association and as a fitting tribute to this great sportsman, the association presented a memorial seat in Hillsborough Park so that their own champion would never be forgotten.

BRUCE WOODCOCK

Of all the boxers to come out of Yorkshire, the most popular has to have been Bruce Woodcock. His popularity was such that Henry Cooper and Frank Bruno have only rivalled him in recent years as the popular British heavyweight of all time, and don't forget that in Bruce's era there was no television to help him achieve a national following.

Born in Doncaster in 1920, one of four brothers, young Bruce was familiar with the boxing ring by the time he was six. Appearing with his mate, Mickey Glennon and billed as 'the mighty midgets', the youngsters gave displays around the South Yorkshire clubs and small halls. After leaving Oswin Avenue School, Bruce took a job with LNER and, aged fourteen, he made his first appearance on a bill as an official representative of the LNER boxing club at Doncaster Corn Exchange. Billed as 'Boy Woodcock, Schoolboy champion of Doncaster, 1933', Bruce beat the schools' champion of York in a four round contest. By the time he was eighteen young Woodcock was boxing as a middleweight and light heavyweight.

In 1938 he won the Northern Counties cruiserweight title at the Tower Circus, Blackpool. After that success, progress was swift and early in 1939 Bruce journeyed to London for the ABA finals and, despite being unlucky in the draw (he was the only quarter-finalist not to get a bye), the young Yorkshireman returned home as ABA light heavyweight champion.

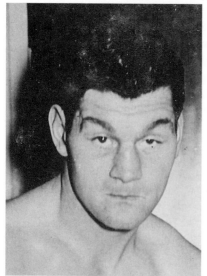

With the advent of war Bruce was considered to be doing too important a job to be drafted. Instead he was sent to work in Manchester. The move to Manchester railway sheds was the turning point in his career. Seeking advice on training facilities, he came into contact with Tom Hurst, who was to be his manager and adviser in his meteoric rise to glory in the fight game.

Bruce made his professional debut at the age of twenty-two, at the Royal

Albert Hall, the setting of his ABA triumph. His opponent was ex-stoker Fred Clarke of London. At the weigh-in Bruce was 12 stone 8lb, while Clarke weighed in at 14 stone 6lb. The heavyweight didn't deter Bruce and Clarke only survived three rounds. In only his seventh professional fight, Bruce became Northern Area Cruiserweight Champion when he beat Jack Robinson of Nottingham inside the distance at Belle Vue. The seven fights in eight months had only lasted a total of twenty-one rounds and Bruce Woodcock was already a name to watch.

Bruce was again based in Doncaster. The Manchester job had finished, enabling him to move back to the depot in his home town. The good form continued and among Bruce's victories were a three round knockout over Arnold Hayes, the heavyweight champion of the Canadian army, a four round fight against George Muir of New Zealand at the London Casino and a win over Les Munden on the Freddie Mills versus Len Harvey, British and British Empire cruiserweight title fight at White Hart Lane. There was talk of Bruce challenging Mills, but manager Hurst was in no hurry to put the Doncaster boy in with the champion.

It was experience that Bruce was after and in his two fights with Glen Moody, the Welshman, he gained just that. The much older Moody, who came from such a distinguished boxing family, was finally overwhelmed by the sheer volume of punches in both matches, but not before he had taught Woodcock a few lessons in ring guile.

The next step on the ladder was a clash with Salford's Tom Reddington at Belle Vue in December 1944. Reddington had already built up a big reputation for himself with three great fights with Freddie Mills, two of which had gone the full distance of ten rounds. Each man had a points verdict and in the third fight the referee had stopped the show in the ninth round in favour of Mills. The fight had only been going two rounds when Bruce, for the first time in his career, found himself decked and twice in a round at that! Boxing carefully, ground was made back in the next two rounds and by the fifth the opening came. Reddington did well to survive the round after taking counts, but by the next round it was all over, a succession of punches terminating his challenge.

The successful run continued and the next set of victories were over Ken Shaw of Dundee, where the referee stopped the fight, Bert Gilroy, also of Scotland, knocked out in the sixth round, Joe Quigley, when the referee stopped the fight in the second round and George Markwick the ex-British army champion, when again the referee intervened and stopped it in the third round.

Bruce's next win, over Canadian Al Delaney, the man Joe Louis said had hit him the hardest of any fighter he had encountered, put his name forward as an official challenger to Freddie Mills. But instead of going for the light heavyweight title, the shrewd Hurst elected to try for Jack London, the British heavyweight champion. Jack London, father of future champion Brian, was eight years older and weighed in at 15 stone 5lb, compared to Bruce at 13 stone. The match was set for fifteen rounds (Woodcock's first at fifteen), at White Hart Lane in a Jack Solomon's open-air promotion in July 1945.

It seemed as though all Doncaster wanted to travel to see their hero in action. Five hundred came from the LNER shop alone, which was obliged to close for the occasion. The first few rounds were very even, the heavier London unable to get in at close quarters. In the fifth, London became stronger and a right on the nose drew blood and for the first time Bruce was driven to the ropes. With renewed determination, Bruce came out for the sixth and almost immediately London went down. A right cross to the head put him down again and again London beat the count but it was obvious the fight was all but over. Another right and London's title had gone. To the echoes of 'Ilkley Moor ba tat', a new champion was crowned, the first Yorkshireman since 'Iron' Hague to win the heavyweight title.

Two more wins, both in three rounds against Bert Gilroy and George James and Bruce was ready to try his luck in America. Madison Square Garden, the legendary New York boxing venue was a far cry from the mighty midgets in Doncaster, but Bruce had come that far and America was the pinnacle in any boxing career. Bruce's opponent was Tami Mauriello, a veteran of seventy-five fights with only seven defeats, two of which had been against Gus Lesnevich for the World Light Heavyweight title. The fight was a bad experience for Bruce. Not only did he lose his 100 per cent record but also he lost the chance of some big pay dates in the States. A clash of heads in the fifth round was the beginning of the end for Woodcock. It left him in a dazed condition and made him an easy victim for the American's

A bloodied **Bruce Woodcock** lands a telling right cross on Lee Savold during their World title fight.

punches which eventually saw Bruce counted out. The cost of the trip was five stitches in a head wound and a swollen knee, but Bruce also had other worries. Three weeks later he was meeting Freddie Mills.

In a match with no titles at stake, Bruce's fight with Mills, surprisingly went the 12 round distance. It was new ground for Woodcock, going so long in a fight and boxing purely on instructions; he opted for a sure points win. Despite heavy criticism for not putting Freddie away, for twice during the match it appeared as if Mills, was ready to go, Bruce's handlers were pleased with the outcome. It was a case of safety first tactics after the debacle in America.

In his next fight Bruce won the European heavyweight championship at his favourite hunting ground Belle Vue. The match was the first to be fought for the European title since the European boxing union had come into being. The Frenchman, Al Renet, was a southpaw, the only 'leftie' Bruce ever fought. After adjusting to Renet's style, Bruce's punishing power finished the fight in the sixth round.

Jack Solomons' next big fight promotion was to put Bruce in with Gus Lesnevich, who had beaten Freddie Mills and was the holder of the World Light Heavyweight title. Although a non-title fight, it was another sell-out and the bookies made the American a favourite, especially as he had beaten Woodcock's only victor Mauriello on two occasions. It was a tough fight as everyone knew it would be from Mills' previous attempt at Lesnevich in the capital. With the Harringay crowd firmly on his side, Bruce's punches gradually wore the American down and to the crowd's great delight, Lesnevich was knocked out in the eighth.

Two European victories over Frenchman Georges Martin at Belle Vue and Swede Nisse Anderson at Harringay and Bruce was ready to meet his next American, Joe Baksi. Roughhouse Baksi had already made his British debut and had outpunched Freddie Mills in six rounds. Baksi, highly rated in America, had title aspirations and Solomons and his cohorts were after American prestige after the Maurillo debacle. Before the fight as a warm up Bruce defended his European title against the Polish born Frenchman, Stephen Alck and gave a very lack-lustre performance, winning on points. The fight with Baksi proved to be Bruce's most disastrous. He opened the first round by falling to a sucker punch which resulted in making the rest of the fight terribly one-sided. Only sheer guts enabled Bruce to last as long as he did. His pleading with Tom Hurst for just another round finally ran out when the referee intervened after seven rounds. It was revealed that Baksi had hit Bruce so hard that he had shattered his jaw. This had happened in the first round and Bruce had fought another six rounds with this painful injury. Bits of broken bone were even found in Bruce's eye, which put him out of action for a while.

This period of inactivity was further extended to allow treatment for a detached retina. Bruce was never the same man after this punishing fight. Perhaps only once, in the Mills return match, did he ever give the boxing display the crowds had been accustomed to seeing.

After a long lay off, Bruce came back in September 1948 to tackle American Lee Oma at a Jack Solomons' Harringay promotion. Oma had had an up and down career, but had beaten Bruce's previous American opponents Mauriello, Baksi and Lesnevich. As now seemed usual the Harringay 10,000 arena was sold out before the night and black-market prices for seats roared to ridiculous heights. The classic fight which seemed so certain, turned out to be a flop owing to Oma being sadly out of condition. Bruce's four round knockout led to severe criticism and there was even groundless speculation of the fight had been fixed.

Jack Solomons, so eager to put a British fighter forward for Joe Louis' title, brought another top ranking American over three months later for Bruce's next match at Harringay. Once again there was an unsatisfactory ending to the contest. Bruce's opponent, Lee Savold, was disqualified for a foul blow in the fourth round. The four rounds leading up to disqualification had seen both men on the canvas. After being warned twice for low blows, the end came when Savold's right caught Woodcock in the groin, sending him to the boards twisting with pain.

Ezzard Charles had assumed Joe Louis' world crown in 1949 but had failed to win worldwide recognition. Solomons immediately matched Bruce and Freddie Mills for Bruce's British, European and British Empire heavyweight titles and billed the fight as an eliminator for the world title, with the aim of making the contest the greatest outdoor show ever.

The second match with Mills was fixed for White City stadium on 2 June 1949. Freddie was now sporting the title World Lightheavyweight Champion, having won the honour a year previously from Lesnevich. Freddie had made a previous attempt in 1944 for the British heavyweight title against Jack London, and had been beaten on points. Due to the lack of light heavyweight challenges, he was never called on to defend his British title, thus being denied the chance to make a Lonsdale Belt his own in the eight years he was champion. Consequently he was obliged to campaign against heavyweights.

Before the fight Bruce went to South Africa, where in defence of his Empire title he beat Johnny Ralph in three rounds.

In front of a 46,000 crowd, Bruce gave what he always considered to be his best match, finally forcing the lion-hearted ever-game Mills to retire in the fourteenth round.

The scene was set for a world title fight, but before Bruce could meet the other contender Lee Savold injuries received in a car accident put him out of action for nine months. Solomons looked at several venues including Bradford's Odsal Stadium, before settling

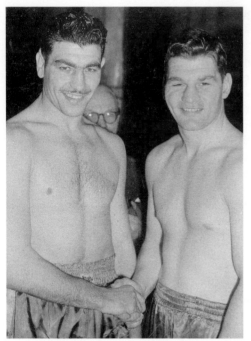

Bruce and Jack Gardner shake hands before Bruce's last fight, a defence of his British Heavyweight title.

for White City again and when Bruce stepped into the ring in June 1950 to meet Savold, he was cheered on by 60,000 eager boxing fans. The fight was recognised by the British Boxing Board of Control as being for the world heavyweight title.

Charles was accepted as champion in the rest of the world, with the position finally clarifying itself when he beat Louis later in 1950, after Louis had beaten Woodcock's conqueror Savold. The fight was over at the end of round four. At the start of the round Savold immediately clinched and, as they broke, a blow to Bruce's right eye saw blood streaming down his face. A desperate effort to finish it only left him open and as the round concluded Hurst's only choice was to throw in the towel.

There was one more fight for Bruce Woodcock, a defence of his title against Jack Gardner, the Leicestershire heavyweight; Bruce's eyes gave in again. The injury that Baksi had given him had made his eyes suspect and at the risk of inoperable damage, Bruce retired after eleven rounds, giving Gardner the British title and another title, the only British fighter ever to beat Bruce Woodcock.

On his retirement Bruce let boxing take a back seat. Among his business ventures was a haulage contracting business and later still he became a publican. Like many fighters Bruce's career in the ring had left its mark and before his death in the late 1990s, Bruce was practically blind.

The late 1940s and early 1950s under Jack Solomons' promotions was a golden era in British boxing and Yorkshiremen can be proud that Doncaster's Bruce Woodcock played a big part in making it so.

BILLY THOMPSON

The second South Yorkshire Boxer to win the British Lightweight title, was Hickleton Main's Billy Thompson, who, in his proud career, became the European champion and the holder of a Lonsdale Belt.

The Thompson's moved to Yorkshire in the early thirties from the Northeast. Billy's father got a job in the area and at the time of the move, young Billy was four years old. His early interest in boxing was developed from his father who was a keen boxing enthusiast. This encouragement started to bear fruit when Billy became schoolboy champion in 1938 and 1939. After leaving Thurnscoe Hill School in 1940, he went the accepted way of most lads in South Yorkshire and went down the pit. Boxing still took up his leisure time and Billy and his father were instrumental in forming an amateur club at Hickleton Main Colliery, Billy remaining with the club throughout his amateur career.

He won the Northern Area title at both bantam and feather weight, which he followed with the lightweight title in 1944. Because of the war, the ABA finals were held at Belle Vue and Thompson, improving all the time, won the lightweight title. Following his ABA success, the next move was to turn professional, which he did and Billy joined the Jervis Astaire, management in London.

Dick Gutteridge, father of TV commentator Reg, became his trainer and Billy moved to the capital, staying with the Gutteridge family and the then lesser known Mickey Duff.

After winning his proffesional fight against Billy Cunningham at Seymour Hall, Billy quickly strung together twenty-odd victories, to push his name forward as a contender for the lightweight title.

His victories included double wins over Belgian, Jose Preys and Claude Dennington, who had been his opponent in the ABA final. Stan Hawthorne, a former rival from his amateur days was matched against Billy at Anfield, football ground in a title eliminator. Hawthorne pulled out all the stops in front of his home crowd and the young Thompson suffered his first professional defeat.

During 1946, Billy became dissatisfied with Astaire as his manager, moving over to Benny Hunt, an associate of Jack Solomons. Dick Gutteridge still continued to be his trainer.

Thurnscoe's **Billy Thompson,** British Lightweight Champion 1947-51.

In 1947, the British Lightweight title became vacant. Welshman Ronnie James had won the title off Eric Boon in 1944, but had never defended it. There was doubt about him being able to make the weight, especially as he was fighting more often in the welterweight class. The British Boxing Board of Control stipulated that he should make 9 stone 12lb (3lb over the lightweight limit) for a contest with Cliff Curvis in June 1947. After he had failed to do so, the Board stripped him of the title and named Thompson and his old rival, Hawthorne, to fight for the title. Hawthorne, who was actually from North Shields and like Billy had moved south, was very much a favourite as he had beaten Billy in their earlier match.

The fight was at Anfield, home of Liverpool Football Club, in front of 20,000 fans, including many from Hickleton Main and the surrounding villages.

Billy was a battler and his all-action style threw Hawthorne off his stride. Hawthorne was forced to join in the hammer and tongs proceedings and all talk of the fight going the distance was soon out of the question. By round two, the adopted Yorkshireman was beginning to break through with his sheer volume of punches. It was like being caught in an avalanche from all sides and by the end of the round Hawthorne had taken two counts and was lucky to survive. Round three proved the finish. Hawthorne's eye was in a bad state, causing the referee to stop the contest in favour of Billy Thompson, the new lightweight champion of Great Britain.

After joyous scenes during his return home to his Yorkshire pit village, the new British lightweight champion was in action again a few months later against Italian, Roberto Proietti, for the European title. Proietti had been European champion in 1946 but had relinquished the title. In 1947 Frenchman, Emile Di Cristo, then beat Belgian Joseph Preys (whom Billy had beaten twice) for the vacant title. Kid Dussart, another Belgian, had beaten Di Cristo and then Proietti had returned to retire Dussart. After a gruelling fifteen rounder, Billy took the points verdict to earn his second title in front of an appreciative London audience. Now Billy had his sights set on a third title, the World Lightweight title.

June 1948 saw Billy and his manager visiting America for talks with a view to a fight with the world champion, Ike Williams. A disagreement over the appointment of a neutral referee led to a stalemate and although Billy met Williams socially, the fight never took place. While he was in America, Billy saw the American fight scene at first hand, when he was able to take in the Tony Zale versus Rocky Graziano world middleweight clash.

After returning home, Billy fought the coloured Canadian, Arthur King, for the vacant Empire title at Belle Vue. The Empire title hadn't, in fact, been fought for since 1936. The King fight only lasted seven rounds. In the sixth Billy received a cut over his eye that meant that only do or die efforts in the next round would prevent him being stopped. Billy gave his all, but failed to stop King and as expected the fight was halted in the Canadian's favour. King later had to forfeit the title when he took out American citizenship.

In the next defence of his European title, Frenchman Pierre Montaine held Billy to a draw at White City. Billy's old opponent, Belgian Joseph Preys, was given the next crack at the European title and Billy beat him at Harringay.

The next contender for Billy's British title was the Scottish champion Harry Hughes. Billy agreed to put the European title at stake and the match was fixed in Hughes' backyard, Celtic Park, Scotland. Billy knew what he was taking on travelling to Scotland but there was £3,000 for the winner and that was a lot of money, for a boy with north-east depression origins. It was the same Thompson who had fought Hawthorne and although he was fighting Hughes in a stadium full of shouting 'jocks', the determined champion overwhelmed the challenger, throwing punches from all angles. The fifth round terminated Hughes' challenge, after the Scot had taken several counts.

July 1949 saw Billy lose his European title to Belgian, Kid Dussart. Dussart, an earlier champion, won the match on a disqualification. It was a sore point as far as Billy was concerned. It was bad enough losing his European title on a disqualification for hitting low, but to lose half his £1,000 purse was a double setback. A few months after, Dussart lost his title to Proietti who now had the European title for the third time. Billy met him in London, but his bid was unsuccessful, the Italian retaining his title after a points victory.

Next on the agenda was the defence of his British title and the opportunity to win a Lonsdale Belt outright. In July 1950 Billy met Tommy McGovern, a fighter from his own stable, but who had done all his early boxing in America. The venue was the unlikely greyhound track at Hanley. The fight went the full distance with Thompson in full flow in his customary style. The decision was fairly close but Thompson was the more determined and he finally won that elusive Lonsdale Belt.

On the European scene, Proietti had retired and once again the title was vacant. Billy was matched with Pierre Montana, the Frenchman whom he had beaten earlier. Before the fight Billy had fought in Johannesburg and had lost to the South African champion, Gerald Dryer. The trip to the sun saw Billy come back a little overweight and the effort to get to championship weight for the European match with Montana left the British champion weak. The effect of the serious business of making the weight began to take effect in the mid-fight rounds. Earlier, boxing in his usual all-action aggressive manner, he had held his own with Montana. In the twelfth round Montana floored the tired Thompson and a series of rights saw him suffer the rare experience of being knocked out.

Later in the year Tommy McGovern, who had given Billy a good fight in their last meeting, was sanctioned by the British Boxing Board of Control as the next challenger for Thompson's British title. For quite a while Billy had been having difficulty meeting the lightweight limit and the effects were seen in his previous fight. The day of the clash at Wandsworth Greyhound Stadium saw the champion 4lb over the lightweight limit. The task of losing it to make the fight made him, in his own words 'as weak as a kitten'. The day was a washout in more ways than one! Heavy rain had curtailed the audience and left the turf so soggy that both boxers had to be carried to the ringside. Billy's vulnerability saw him make an indignant exit in one of the shortest ever title fights. He was knocked out in only 45 seconds! Following the resulting suspension by the British Boxing Board of Control, Billy resumed his career after a lengthy break. He moved up permanently to the welterweight class and, although he kept up a winning sequence, he wasn't completely happy with his form. For the first time in his career he was coming away feeling hurt in the ring, so he made the decision to quit at the comparatively early age of twenty-six.

His decision to go out while still on top, without taking any more unnecessary punishment, was a wise one.

One of the most popular boxers ever to step into the ring and well-remembered, not only in Yorkshire, but all over England, Billy Thompson was a credit to his profession.

BILLY CALVERT

During the 1960s one man reigned supreme in the British featherweight ranks and that was Howard Winstone, the talented Welshman who, in the twilight of his ring career, received the accolade of becoming world champion. The honour of coming nearest to beating him belonged to a Sheffield lad called Billy Calvert, who in their fifteen round battle was inches away from dethroning a great champion.

Born in 1933, Billy was seventeen when he first started boxing. Bob Biney, the instructor at the Crookes Boys' School in Sheffield, was the first to put him through his paces. Billy was serving his apprenticeship as a joiner, so his national service was deferred until, at the age of twenty-one, his apprenticeship was completed. Following his call up and initial training, the army posted young Calvert to Singapore, where his boxing career started to blossom. Fighting as a bantam, he won the South-East Asia title in 1955 and 1956, while his greatest honour was boxing for Singapore in the South-East Asia Games when, in competition with other young boxers from another nine countries, he won the gold medal in his class.

After his demob from the army, Billy entered for the ABA championships, but had to withdraw from the 1957 competition due to illness. The following year, still boxing for Crookes Boys' Club, Billy won the Northern Counties title, but was beaten in the ABA semi-finals by Welshman, Malcolm Collins. The match with Collins was a bad experience; Billy considered the result unfair and the occasion proved to be the Sheffield lad's last opportunity

Billy Calvert, Sheffield's popular featherweight of the 1960s.

to win in the ABA championships. Collins went on in the same year to win the British Commonwealth Title at the games in Cardiff.

In the middle of 1958 Billy turned professional, while continuing his partnership with his trainer from his Boys' Club days, Bob Biney. Bob also managed a couple of local lads including Billy's younger brother Ronnie. Billy's professional career started off on the right note for on his paid debut he beat Johnny Fitzpatrick at Doncaster Corn Exchange, stopping him in the second round. Before the year was out the Sheffielder had two more victories to his name, including one over Eric Brett at Nottingham.

The 1959 season started in exactly the same way. By the end of May he had completed points wins over Jerry Parker at Derby, Chris Elliott also at Derby, Brian Jago in his London debut and had beaten Andy Hayford twice, the first at Halifax and the second in his South Yorkshire debut at Rotherham Baths. By now Billy had stepped up to eight rounders and, making his second London appearance, he was beaten by Eddie West.

The next two fights were in Wales. Brian Jago avenged his earlier defeat at Bognor Regis, and Billy had his first encounter with Howard Winstone at Aberdare. Winstone was already making a name for himself (inside two years, he would be British Champion) and the referee had to intervene during round seven to save Billy from further punishment. The run of three defeats came to an end when Billy met Brian Jago at Wembley in October. This was the best of three. Billy had won the first in only his fourth professional fight, but the return match had resulted in a debatable decision and Billy had wanted a third meeting to settle the matter once and for all. This time the decision was clear and after the defeat Jago retired from boxing.

Billy's next victim was Con Mount Bassie of Bournemouth, who was defeated at Carlisle. A week later Billy returned to Wembley and on the night Terry Downes won the British Middleweight Title, Billy beat Hugh O'Neill on points. The decision went against Billy in his fight with John Smillie at Carlisle, but on his next appearance in his own home town, Billy knocked out Terry Rees in two rounds. Calvert's last appearance in 1959 was against Howard Winstone at the National Sporting Club. This time the clash went the full distance and, despite a valiant effort in a very crowd pleasing display, Billy was beaten again.

In March 1960 Billy was matched for the Central Area title against Eddie Burns of Liverpool at Rotherham Baths Hall. Despite an eye injury Billy clinched the title and advanced in the rankings for the British featherweight title.

During the summer of the same year Billy had one of his stiffest challenges to date when he was matched with Percy Lewis, the Empire champion. West Indian Lewis, who was based in England, had been Empire Champion since 1957 and had also, as an amateur, won the ABA featherweight title in 1953. Billy made the most of his opportunity and, in earning a draw with Lewis, he enhanced his chances for a title fight. The following month Olympic Games hero Terry Spinks beat Bobby Neill for the British title, but hovering in the wings waiting for his chance was Howard Winstone.

For Calvert's next fight there was a trip to Rome where the Yorkshireman was beaten on points. It was one of those decisions that adds fuel to the argument that the only way to win in Italy was by knocking out the local fighter. There was also a reversal in Billy's last match of 1960.

He fought Ghana's Love Allotey at Manchester and once again it was a close defeat on points. Allotey had a world rating and usually fought in the lightweight ranks and later in the 1960s he went on to win the Empire crown as a lightweight.

During the year Billy changed managers. His new manager was 'Tiger' Al Phillips, who in 1947 had himself fought for the same featherweight title that Billy was chasing. Phillips' match with the forty-year-old Tarleton had been one of the best remembered fights of all time.

Billy started off 1961 with a win over Roy Jacobs at Liverpool but was beaten in his next outing which was also on Merseyside. Irishman Freddie Gilroy was British and Empire bantam champion and only five months before his fight with Billy, he had lost on points to Alphonse Halimi for the world title in a match in which he had also lost his European title. Billy lost on points the decision was close and the experience valuable. Back on winning terms, Billy beat Phil Jones at Manchester, but was again beaten in Europe, this time by Olli Maki of Finland. In Calvert's words, the Maki fight which took place at Gothenberg, was again very much a hometown decision. Maki later competed as a lightweight and won the European title in 1964.

Before fighting in the top class, Billy's next opponent was Floyd Robertson from Ghana, who had captured Lewis' Empire Title. Robertson was held to a draw at Manchester and to finish off 1961 Billy took part in another draw at London against Mick Greaves.

The first fight of 1962 was against Danny O'Brien, a top rated feather-cum-lightweight and Billy gained an impressive points victory.

After a period of inactivity Billy's comeback fight was a points win

Sheffield blade **Billy Calvert** (left) staggers Empire champ Floyd Robertson with a hard left to the head in their Manchester battle. After ten action-filled rounds the referee gave it a draw.

over American Terry Rand at Leeds. On the same bill was Howard Winstone, now British champion and at that moment in time rated number two in the world. In what was regarded as a warm-up fight for Winstone's European and world title bid, he was suprisingly beaten by American, Leroy Jeffery. The Winstone victory put the former American Golden Gloves champion to number four in the world ranking and three weeks later the strong punching Jeffery, was matched against Billy Calvert. The Sheffield man restored British pride when, in a fight that had the fans on the edge of their seats, he clearly exposed the American and beat him on points. Sadly for Jeffery it was the end of his line. On his return to America he was injured in a car accident and never fought again.

The win over Winstone's victor put Billy at the top of the featherweight ratings and in the following February he was matched against Scottish champion Bobby Fisher in a title eliminator. Glasgow had often been a graveyard for English boxers, but on this occasion Calvert put the result beyond any doubt when he knocked Fisher out in the tenth round.

The title fight with Winstone took place six months later at

Porthcawl. The fight was for the British and European titles, Winstone having won the latter a month earlier in Cardiff. Before the fight Winstone had had four British title fights against Terry Spinks, Derry Treanor, Harry Carroll and Johnny Morrisey and all four had been beaten inside the distance. His fight with Billy was Winstone's hardest battle of his career so far and for the first time he was taken the full fifteen rounds. Billy was a real surprise packet and he hustled and bustled Winstone with non-stop determination and aggression, completely throwing the champion off his stride. Only Winstone's true class when in desperate positions helped the champion thwart Billy's challenge. It was obviously going to be close and when the referee announced the verdict, it was a very disappointed Billy who heard that his challenge was unsuccessful.

This near triumph in his fight for the championship eventually proved to be the peak of Billy's boxing career. While for Winstone there were three unsuccessful challenges for Vincente Salvador's world title, Winstone eventually won the title, when Salvidor retired for a while but he was only champion for six months.

Billy's next fight after his title challenge was against old opponent Con Mount Bassie at Blackburn, a contest which he won on points. A month later Billy met Frenchman Michael Arlan at Wembley. The bout followed the heavyweight clash between Billy Walker and Johnny Prescott. The fight was a regrettable experience. Arlan clearly didn't want to know, but unfortunately a clash of heads which opened a cut near Billy's eye forced his retirement after four uninteresting rounds. The last fight of 1963 was a trip to Accra in Ghana to have a second clash with the Empire champion, Floyd Robertson. The African had improved since their previous meeting and stopped Calvert in seven rounds. Robertson then had a tilt at Salvador's world title but was stopped inside the distance.

1964 proved to be Billy's last year as a professional boxer. His form started to suffer and after a win over Bobby Davies at Sheffield City Hall, and a loss to Brian Cartwright, Billy made a wise decision to step out of the ring for good.

A popular figure at Sheffield's Old Boxers' Association's meetings, Billy was one of boxing's unfortunate men who, if he had been fighting in another era, could well have been an outstanding British champion.

SHAUN DOYLE

Nicknamed 'the blond bombshell', South Yorkshire's popular battler of the 'swinging sixties' was Barnsley born and bred.

Shaun Doyle, who became the first fighter from the town since Chuck Parker in the 1930s to fight for a British title and then later when he turned his hand to promotion, Doyle brought Barnsley its first British Title fight in 1978.

Born in Union Court, Barnsley on the first day of the year 1945, Shaun left Holy Rood School at fifteen to become a miner at North Gawber Colliery. Shaun's father Joseph had been a boxer in his youth and he encouraged his son to follow in his footsteps and don the gloves. Training in the gym at the back of *The Junction Inn*, his potential was quickly spotted by two of Barnsley's favourite boxing sons Joe Birch and Charlie Glover, father of the late sportsman and actor Brian. Other influences were Reg Laybourn, another old boxer and masseur at Barnsley FC and Gordon Wood, a 1930s Barnsley middleweight who trained him.

After only five amateur fights in National Coal Board contests, Shaun turned professional. His last amateur fight against Jackie Turpin had ended in a disqualification for Doyle, for hitting with an open glove.

Boxing as a welterweight Doyle won his first professional contest against Welshman Tommy Waterworth, who had just turned professional himself, after representing his country in the Olympics. Peter Bates, the South Yorkshire boxer who had gained fame in the 1950s when he beat Henry Cooper, became his manager. At this time Shaun also had some encouraging sparring sessions with boxing miner Terry Halpin from Wombwell.

Britain had a great welterweight champion in Brian Curvis, who had been British champion since 1960 and Shaun Doyle's attempt to gain a position from which he could challenge Curvis for title honours gained him some rungs up the ladder, especially when he won the Central Area title at Sheffield in November 1965, beating Gordon McAteer. That win, coupled with a series of others, saw Shaun end the year rated fourth in the list of challengers for Curvis's title. The two main men in front of him were the two scousers Johnny

Barnsley's blond bombshell, **Shaun Doyle.** *(photo loaned by Shaun Doyle).*

Cooke (Bootle) and Brian McCaffrey.

In February the following year Shaun was matched against his first American opponent, James 'Silky' Shelton. In those days fight preparation wasn't what it is today. Only a couple of days before the fight Doyle was quoted in the *Barnsley Chronicle*, as stating that he didn't know a thing about his opponent, whether he was a southpaw, an orthodox or even a black or white American. 'Silky' turned out to be twenty-seven, coloured and six pounds heavier. In his thirty-five fights he had never lost inside the distance. Also he had boxed many times on the continent and had beaten the Italian, Golferini, but lost on points to the rated Nino Benvenuti. Shelton's extra weight seemed to make the difference and Doyle lost the ten round contest at Blackpool Tower on points.

Curvis' manager Arthur Boggis, the meat magnate, had promised Shaun a tilt at the title in the summer of 1966 and the talk was that Oakwell (Barnsley FC ground) would be used for the occasion. After Shaun had recovered from an injury received in his occupation as a scrap dealer, there was talk of a return bout with the American, Shelton, at Sheffield. Cuban Jose Stable, ranked eighth in the world, was also mooted as a possible opponent and there was local clamour around Doncaster for Shaun to face his local rival Fred Powney. The pair had met four times before with the verdicts pretty evenly shared, but Fred had dropped out of the 1965 top welters and so Doyle thought he'd nothing to prove by fighting him again.

Des Rea, the Northern Ireland champion, was only one rating behind Doyle and the pair met a month after the Shelton fight (the return with the American being sidelined). A points win over Rea at Sheffield fuelled the talk of a clash with Curvis who was at that time attempting to get another fight with Emile Griffith, who, he had lost to on points in a world title fight at Wembley in 1964.

Instead of meeting Curvis, Shaun was matched with Johnny Cooke in a June 1966 eliminator for a tilt at the Welshman's title. The bout was to take place at the Anglo-American Sporting Club in London. This was to be Shaun's first fight for his new manager, 'Tiger' Al Phillips (European featherweight champion in the 1940s). Doyle's relationship with Bates had soured, the Barnsley boxer often being critical of Bates for keeping him in 'the dark'. Sheffield boxer, Billy Calvert, was now training Shaun and the party left for London to prepare for the Cooke fight.

It transpired that their former manager Bates had arranged a fight with Ricky Porter who was ranked fifteenth in the welterweight division. An Angry Doyle who claimed he knew nothing of the fight and that Bates hadn't been his manager for some time, was forced to meet Porter after a British Boxing Board of Control inquiry ordered that the contest should go ahead. Shaun talked of handing in his licence over this decision which effectively lost him the title eliminator. Phillips persuaded him to fight and he beat Porter on points. While there was talk of Cooke having a second tilt at Curvis, Shaun, who had reportedly given up his Central Area title, was told to fight Fred Powney. Shaun stated that he had nothing to gain by meeting Powney again. When reports flourished that he was ducking Fred, Doyle agreed to take the fight and for the first time in their five meetings the fight didn't go the distance. Powney was stopped in round seven at the South Staffordshire Social Club at Wolverhampton. To round off 1966, in his next outing Shaun defeated Don McMillan in London, his opponent being another fighter in the top ten ratings.

When Brian Curvis announced his retirement, Johnny Cooke, at thirty-two, won the vacant title when he beat number one challenger, Brian McCaffrey in February 1967. The same month Shaun beat Gilles Fincanto on points at Nottingham, before the news broke that Shaun Doyle at twenty-two was to be Cooke's challenger in the first defence of his new British title.

Yorkshire Traction laid buses on as Doyle's faithful Barnsley followers travelled to Cooke's backyard at Liverpool Stadium. 'Tiger' Al Phillips was forecasting a win for his ten year younger man by the fight's halfway stage, whilst Cooke's manager, Johnny Campbell, was quoted as saying that all Doyle was, was just a strong kid. Promoter Selwyn Demmy was wanting to match the winner against McCaffrey later in the year, with the winner of that bout to meet European Jean Josselin, who had retired Curvis in thirteen rounds in April 1966. Experience proved the key as Cooke won the fight on points. Doyle gave everything he had as his Barnsley fans knew he would, but only briefly did the never-say-die, durable Yorkshire lad give any indication that his sheer strength might enable him to overcome the superior ring craft and experience of the champion. The occasion was in the fourth and fifth rounds, when Cooke momentarily forsook his strict defensive counter-punching methods, opting for an all-out attack. In the seventh Doyle seemed to worry Cooke who had a cut, but the champion eventually fought his way out of trouble. Despite his failure to beat the champion, Doyle received a good reception from the home crowd, especially when it was revealed that referee Harry Gibbs had made Cooke the winner by only half a point, with Cooke winning seven rounds, Doyle four and the rest even.

After a couple of postponements, including one against the Anglo-Pakistani Evan Whiter at Nottingham, when Shaun withdrew with an injured foot, Doyle's next fight was against Londoner Peter Cragg, a former ABA champion. Cragg, since turning professional, had won all his first twelve fights inside the distance. The contest took place at

Shaun ducks low to get in a challenge. *(photo loaned by Shaun Doyle)*

the Seymour Hall, London and for the first time in his twenty-seven fight career, Doyle was stopped. Even though he was still on his feet, the referee stopped the fight because in his opinion Shaun had already taken too much punishment. The papers slated the decision by the referee as being premature and an upset Shaun ranted that Cragg was on the verge of punching himself out and though he, Shaun, had been down, he had risen immediately.

Shaun lost his interest in boxing after that decision.

He knew his chances of another title challenge were remote, for the defeats had seen him drop from third to eighth in the British ratings and besides Cragg, there were other up and coming challengers like West Ham's Ralph Charles rising through the welter ranks.

The Barnsley man retired in his mid-twenties with only a handful of defeats in just under thirty professional fights.

Champion Cooke lost the title in February 1968 to Ralph Charles, after which he carried on into his late thirties losing more fights than he was winning. One man who beat him twice was Les Pearson from Pontefract, one of the occasions being for the Central Area title in 1971.

Shaun Doyle followed a well-trodden path for ex-boxers and moved into the public house business, becoming licensee at *The Plough* in Doncaster Road. He also became a boxing promoter in the area and in 1976 was instrumental in bringing Barnsley its first British title fight when Henry Rhiney fought Billy Waith at the Civic Hall for the same welterweight crown he himself and Chuck Parker had tried to bring to their hometown.

Whilst maintaining his interest in boxing, particularly in any promising youngster, Shaun built himself an empire in the security business and after having to live with the tragedy of losing one of his sons in a motor cycle accident, has passed most of the business on to the other son.

Not a boxer in the mould of some of the South Yorkshire champions, but a tough fighting customer in the ring, he was as pleased as punch when another Barsnley boxer came to the fore in the 1990s in the shape of Chris Saunders, who was destined to win the British Welterweight title at the third attempt by a Barnsley boxer.

ALLAN RICHARDSON

Yorkshire's boxing star of the 1970s was the stylish little battler Allan Richardson. The Yorkshire mining village of Fitzwilliam has produced several famous sons, Geoff Boycott instantly springing to mind, and in carrying on the tradition, the village produced a British champion at both amateur and professional levels, a champion stocked with Yorkshire grit and determination.

When Allan, who was born in 1945, was eight years old, his father took him to the local miners' welfare training club and the youngster promptly followed the example of his two brothers who had previously donned the gloves. However, Allan was not really keen on boxing at this period, he fancied himself more as a rugby league player. Nonetheless he was encouraged to embark upon an amateur boxing career, which proved no easy path, and for a while it was considered that he was too short to be taken seriously. Fitness and courage played a big part during the majority of his early fights, many of which were rugged battles. Never a big puncher, Allan had an immaculate left hand in the finest boxing traditions, which when coupled with his courage and commitment, made him a formidable opponent.

In 1968 in the ABA championships, the Yorkshire boxer reached the semi-final before losing to Johnny Cheshire, a London based Scot. The following year Allan became ABA featherweight champion when he defeated Eddie Richard of Menai Bridge in the final.

In 1970 the Commonwealth Games were held in Edinburgh and Richardson was delighted to be picked as the English featherweight participant. The year before Allan had lost his ABA title to Scot Ian Cameron. It was sweet revenge when the Yorkshire boxer met the local favourite in the quarter-final, with the win over Cameron assuring him of a medal. Allan's semi-final opponent was Philip Waruingue from Kenya. The Kenyan was too experienced for him and Allan had to settle for the bronze medal as the losing semi-finalist.

Following a tour of America with an English amateur boxing team, there was an offer on the table for him to turn professional. A demanding fight programme and a series of hard rugged fights had

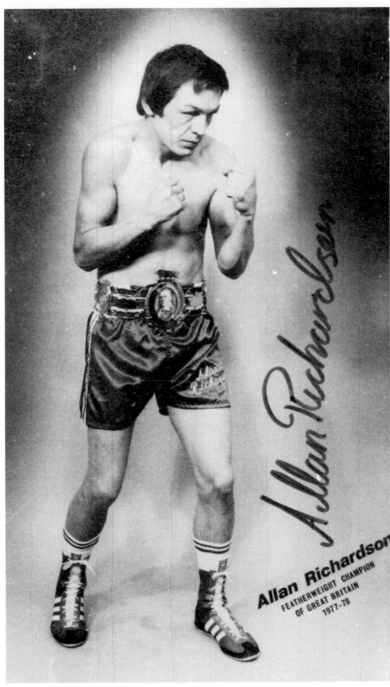

Allan Richardson, Featherweight Champion of Great Britain 1977-78.

made their mark and before Allan could turn professional, the British Boxing Board of Control, made him wait almost a year before passing him fit to commence his professional career.

Allan signed up with Yorkshire manager Trevor Calligham from Wyke, near Bradford, whose own background was in rugby league as a player and director with Dewsbury. Commencing as a professional in late 1971, Allan finished the year off winning his first two professional fights. In the following year, the next four fights went the same way. Bingo Crook and Sammy Vernon were both beaten on points at Manchester, Dave Tuohey lasted only three rounds at the same venue, and in his sixth professional fight and his first eight rounder Nick Gawai was beaten on points at Liverpool. In September Allan dropped his first decision when Billy Hardacre beat him on points in Manchester. In his last fight of 1972 Allan drew with Billy Waith at Leeds (Waith a few years later would fight for the welter title).

During 1973 Allan only fought four times, winning three. The most important win was a revenge victory over Billy Hardcastle for the Central Area title. The points win earned him a tilt at the British featherweight title, for the Board had sanctioned the area fight as an eliminator.

The British champion was Scot Evan Armstrong, who had beaten Jimmy Revie in 1971 to win the title, which he lost after a year to fellow Scot Tommy Glencross, winning it back it the following year.

The 31-year-old skinny-ribbed champion was very much the favourite and before the fight he had beaten Vernon Sollas, the other main challenger. Over 200 supporters travelled from Fitzwilliam to see the 25-year-old coal fitter challenge for the championship at the World's Sporting Club, London in July 1974. It was a truly memorable fight and was later voted as one of the fights of the year. It proved unlucky thirteen for Allan, for in his thirteenth paid fight Richardson gave a tremendous display of guts and determination, proving himself worthy of the occasion. He did particularly well after weathering a storm in the seventh when the Scot forced the action after Allan had been floored. By the tenth round, Allan was ahead on points, although both men were bleeding from cuts obtained earlier in the fight. At the end of the round Armstrong strode to his corner utterly dejected. Richardson's stamina was unbreakable and unless Armstrong came back more into the fight the championship would have a new owner. The next round proved the turning-point and it seemed as if Armstrong's prayer had been answered. A savage left hook which hit Richardson flush on the chin, knocked him completely off his feet. Although the Yorkshireman was quick to get up, in no way was he fit to continue and referee Harry Gibbs had no hesitation in stopping the contest and holding Armstrong's hand up. The title fight with Armstrong being Allan's only fight in 1974.

Allan's career was resumed in January 1975 when he beat Danny Fearnon at the National Sporting Club (London). The following month he met Vernon Sollas at the Royal Albert Hall. Armstrong, on winning his Lonsdale Belt outright, had retired and Allan and Sollas were matched in a title eliminator. Sollas, whose form in his overall career was very unpredictable, was at this moment very much the man to beat. Sollas beat Allan on the day, stopping him in eight rounds and then going on in the following month to win the vacant Featherweight title, beating Jimmy Revie in only four rounds.

Allan went on to finish the year with a win and a loss. He beat Colin Miles on points at the National Sporting Club and lost on points to Belgian Ferrard Roelands at Bruges. The Belgian affair was highly criticised as being a hometown decision, with the Richardson management amazed that their man had been beaten. The Yorkshireman put himself back in contention for another title chance when he stopped the Scottish champion, Gerry Duffy, in six rounds and then beat the former British bantam champion Dave Needham in three.

In the two years since winning the title, Sollas had not defended it until Allan was given another chance in March 1977. The promoters, with sufficient local interest being shown in the man from Fitzwilliam, secured the fight for Leeds. It had been forty years since Yorkshire had held a British title fight, the previous occasion being the Len Hampston versus Johnny King bantam clash at Headingley in 1938.

Sollas had shown a loss of form since becoming champion and only a month before his clash with Richardson, he had been stopped by Welshman Les Pickett. The winner had been in trouble in the first four rounds, surviving a knockout before coming back in the later stages to win the fight. The Scot had also challenged for the European title and lost in similar circumstances. The pre-fight talk considered the Yorkshireman was in with a chance if he could survive Sollas' early onslaught. The Scot's notorious habit of losing concentration and running out of steam as the fight reached the later stages would suit Allan who himself was a slow starter, but was also one of the bravest boxers in the business who could be assured of giving his all in front of his own supporters.

As he entered the Leeds Town Hall for his second title challenge

Allan's record stood at fifteen wins in twenty-one fights. There was a lucrative bonus for the winner, for the Empire title was vacant and there was an offer of £6,000 for the British champion, to fight Nigerian Eddie Ndukwu in Lagos. Sollas had been keen to accept the fight with Ndukwu, but the Board had first ordered the defence of his home title. The fight took the expected early course with Sollas winning the opening rounds. Gradually Richardson's non-stop aggression started to pay dividends and more and more punches started to penetrate the Scot's defence. The fight was at the halfway stage when the Yorkshireman's sheer volume of punching started to have the required effect. The frustrated Sollas was cautioned several times for butting and it was obvious he was gradually losing heart. By the eighth round the referee had no alternative but to award the belt to Richardson as the champion was no longer in a condition to defend himself.

Allan Richardson's display made him the first Tyke to hold the featherweight crown since Sheffield's Johnny Cuthbert in the late 1920s. It was the end for Vernon Sollas, for in the same year the British Boxing Board of Control took away his licence after he had been stopped three times in succession.

Three months after his title win, Allan attempted to win his second title when he travelled to Nigeria to meet Eddie Ndukwu for the vacant British Empire and Commonwealth titles. Unbeaten as a professional Ndukwu had won the gold medal in the 1974 Commonwealth games in New Zealand. The match attracted great interest in Africa and it was expected that 100,000 people would witness the affair at the Nigerian National Stadium in Lagos. Heavy rain curtailed the promotion and the Nigerians wanted to postpone for twenty-four hours. Calligham refused on the grounds that a postponement would affect his boxer's preparation and the fight went ahead as arranged. As it was, only 15,000 turned out to see what became a great fight. Ndukwu proved to be a good challenger, with Allan surviving until the twelfth round when a right cross floored him. The odds had been stacked against him, for he had survived earlier counts in the second and third rounds, but showing his usual bravery, he had come back and given the African a good battle.

In October 1977, Allan travelled to Wales to defend his featherweight title against Les Pickett. The fight was a terrifically close affair with Allan winning on points. This fight was the first in which Richardson had gone the full fifteen rounds and the Welshman, in front of his own fans, had given him the hardest fight of his career. The winning point margin was 144-145. Victorous, Allan returned home £5,000 richer and now with two notches on his Lonsdale Belt. Six months later, former bantam champion, Dave Needham from Nottingham, was matched with Allan for the title and this time the bout was fought in London at the Worlds Sporting Club. Allan's reign as champion came to an end after thirteen months when the southpaw Needham out punched him. As usual, Richardson started late and as the fight went on he launched upon several desperate exchanges in an effort to save his title, but Needham seemed to be swarming all over him and he failed to stop the challenger who grew in stature as the fight progressed. In the bloody encounter, Allan had put Needham down in the ninth round, although the challenger's camp claimed a low punch. After the fight had finished and Needham had won the very hard fought match, it was revealed that Richardson had been handicapped by a damaged left hand for half the fight. Despite the handicap, Allan duly acknowledged his victor, there being no way the former champion wanted to use the injured hand as an excuse.

There was only one more fight for Allan Richardson, another bid for Ndukwu's Empire title, which proved unsuccessful and in October 1978, the brave little Yorkshireman duly announced his retirement. Boxing wasn't finished with entirely, with an interest in schoolboy action and attendance at Old Boxers' Association events keeping his hand in. Also, he was able to pursue his other sporting love, cricket, opening the batting for one of his local teams, Hemsworth Miners Welfare.

There have been some great British champions from South Yorkshire, few if any braver than Allan Richardson, a fine example of true Yorkshire grit.

BRIAN ANDERSON

During the 1980s it was an Irishman who, after the lean years following the Second World War, made Sheffield a major rival to the other northern boxing cities of Liverpool and Manchester.

Dubliner Brendan Ingle, who campaigned in the early 1970s as a middleweight in the city (he was good enough to be in the top ten British ratings in 1973), was instrumental in bringing Sheffield its first British title fight for sixty years in 1978, when lightweight Colin Power beat Chris Walker, the Sheffield based, Retford born challenger. But it is as a manager that Ingle achieved his greatest fame, first with Herol 'Bomber' Graham and more lately with Sheffield's own prince, the flamboyant Prince Naseem.

Unlucky to be around at the same time as his stablemate Graham, and therefore in his shadow for the majority of his career, Brian Anderson proved his own class when he followed Herol in the highly competitive middleweight division, to become British champion in 1986. And acknowledging the fact that Graham was born in Nottingham, and Roly Todd who won the title in the mid 1920s was from the north-east, Brian was the first Yorkshireman to win the middleweight title for sixty-six years.

Tall for a middleweight at 6ft 1in, Brian was born in Sheffield in 1961. Always in scrapes at school, the logical thinking was to apply his aggression to the boxing ring and Brian first donned the gloves at the age of fourteen. After three years at Croft, his home amateur club, he moved to Eckington where the tall teenager won a NABC title. Spotted by Ingle, who was always impressed with his fighter's dedication, Brian signed for the former building worker and adopted Yorkshireman. Brendan's wife Alma had joined him in the boxing world and as well as taking part in the promotion of the sport, she became the first woman to be elected to a British Boxing Board, when she joined the Central Area committee in Manchester.

Put through his paces by Brendan at his St Thomas' Church Hall gym, Brian's professional debut came at Manchester in April 1980, when he recorded a six round points win over Jeff Standley. After a second win at Liverpool against Jeff Aspell, there was controversy in

Brian Anderson of Sheffield. British Middleweight Champion 1986.

Anderson's third fight when the Sheffielder was disqualified in round four of his fight against Dave Ward for biting. Brian fumed afterwards that his opponent had head butted him and had taken the first bite and in his opinion Ward had been lucky to escape being spotted by the referee. In what was proving not to be a good start to his career, Brian lost his next outing against Cliff Gilpin at Wolverhampton. It was Gilpin's fifth professional fight and the Wolverhampton boxer, who was really a welter-cum-light middleweight, took his unbeaten run to thirteen wins before Kirkland Laing stopped him twice on points. In 1983, in an eight month period, Gilpin went the twelve round distance twice with Lloyd Honeyghan for the British Welterweight Title.

After two draws which meant his professional start had realised only two wins out of six fights, Brian's form improved and he put together an unbeaten series of wins, so that by the time 1981 ended his new record showed a more impressive sixteen fights, eleven wins, three draws and two defeats. His sixteenth fight had been his first abroad and he had beaten Eckhard Dagge, who had been European champion in the mid-1970s, in West Germany and in two rounds at that. With 'Bomber' ending 1981 unbeaten in nineteen fights and a big favourite in Sheffield, where half his wins had taken place and where, strangely enough, Brian had still to make his hometown debut, there was considerable speculation that the two stablemates would meet in the future and no one was looking forward to it more than Brendan Ingle.

To keep busy, in January 1982 Brian went back to Germany, taking a fight at three hours' notice against Frank Wissenbach, and losing on points. That defeat spoiled a lengthy unbeaten run, for Anderson didn't lose another fight that year and chalked up two winning Sheffield appearances. Brian's long awaited Sheffield debut was against Pat Thomas at the Crucible. Thomas was his best rated British opponent to date, for the Welshman had been a double champion winning both British welter and light middleweight titles. There was an opportunity to compare himself with Graham against the same opponent, for Herol had beaten Thomas in a fifteen round points decision a year earlier to win his light middle crown. Anderson had sparred with Ayub Kayule and Welshman Colin Jones and it was obvious his defensive technique had improved since his workouts with 'Bomber'. Thomas didn't win a round and it looked as if Brian could have finished it in the sixth. Ingle kept him on a tight rein, with consistent punching building up a comfortable points lead which culminated in a convincing win.

The possibility of a title clash with Graham came a step nearer when in his second fight in Sheffield, Brian beat another Cardiff boxer Darwin Brewster in an eliminating contest for a tilt at Herol's title. The pair had met before, drawing in Anderson's twelfth professional fight and Brewster's fourth, after the Welshman had started his career with three straight wins. Before the second meeting Brewster, who had been an ABA winner in 1979, had lost only two fights in eleven appearances. Both his defeats had been against non-British boxers. Brewster had lost to John Mugabi, the 1980 Olympic medalist, whom noone else would fight, and Ace Ruseviki at a venue in Yugoslavia. Referee John Coyle only gave Brewster one round as Brian swept to a decisive ten round points victory at the Top Rank Suite. Anderson commanded from the first bell as the Sheffield crowd got behind their local hero. Anderson was now to meet the winner of the Prince Rodney (Huddersfield) and Graeme Ahmed (South Shields) clash in a final eliminator.

A fortnight later Rodney, managed by Maurice Hope the former World champion and one time holder of the British Light Middleweight title, beat Ahmed in three rounds at Middlesbrough avenging an earlier defeat to clinch his fight with Anderson. As Rodney was Central Area light middle champion, that title was also put up. Rodney's record was twenty-five wins from thirty-two contests.

The fight, Anderson's third successive hometown bout, took place on 14 March 1983, after two earlier dates had been cancelled due to Rodney having the 'flu. Rodney, who was London born but Huddersfield based, had met Graham two years earlier and had been embarrassingly beaten in one round in a non-title fight. Prince Rodney proved the better man on the night and for the first time Brian was stopped, the referee terminating the fight in round five. While Brian was left to reflect on what might have been, Rodney didn't meet Graham; he had relinquished his title to move onto the more attractive full middleweight division. Prince Rodney became champion when he beat Jimmy Batten for the vacant title at the Royal Albert Hall in October 1983.

Big Brian bounced back in the best possible way when he beat Ahmed in five rounds in his own backyard the next month. Brian too began to campaign in the middleweight ranks and in May 1983 he beat Jimmy Everhard Ellis for the vacant Central Area middleweight title. Ellis, another fighter on Brendan Ingle's books who also fought as light heavyweight, had boxed a draw with scouser Sammy Brennan for the vacant title, only the week before his fight with Anderson.

Naturally, Brennan was given his chance with Anderson, who prior to their meeting in Spring 1984, had beaten Doug James in one round and dropped a points decision to Andrea Mongalema in France. Brennan was beaten in one round and after a points win in Sheffield over Winston Burnett, Anderson enjoyed a trip to Brisbane to record a ten round points win over Emmanuel Otti.

Chris Pyatt, with an excellent amateur record which included a Commonwealth games medal and an ABA Welterweight Title in 1982 was the up and comer in the light middleweight ranks. Pyatt, who had defeated Brewster and retired Pat Thomas, had won all his eleven professional fights and was matched with Brian in an eliminator for the light middleweight title which was held by Jimmy Cable, who had won the vacant title after Rodney had failed to defend it. Pyatt was hot and he took the points verdict in front of his own Leicester crowd. By the time Pyatt got his chance to fight for the title a year later, it was owned by Rodney again, who had regained it from Jimmy Cable.

For the next year Brian fought mostly Europeans with contests in Germany and France. When his mate Herol announced he was giving up his British middleweight title which he had won in April 1985 to chase world honours, Brian was matched with Liverpool based Steve Johnson in a Central Area defence and eliminator for the vacant title. Johnson, though a professional since 1982, had only taken part in half the contests Anderson had. The Sheffield boxer's thirty-sixth fight saw him gain the chance to fight for a British title at last, after he stopped Johnson in five rounds.

For the title, Brian met the Southern Area champion, Londoner Tony Burke, whose record was sixteen fights and four defeats. Prior to the fight, Brian made his fourth appearance in France. The big man had never any luck in that country, his only win there coming against Gratian Tonna and, for the second time in his career, Brian was stopped when the referee ended it in round eight in favour of his opponent Frank Winterstein.

The bout for the British middleweight title was held at the Ulster Hall, Belfast. Experience told as Anderson finished the job in six rounds to give Sheffield another British champion and put Brendan Ingle up another rung on his way to the top of the managerial ladder.

After a career in which he had fought on a very regular basis, it was nearly a year before Brian defended his title. His opponent was a British boxing legend, Tony Sibson, another of Leicester's great ring men. 'Sibbo' had done everything. Still not thirty, his record was fifty-four wins from sixty-one fights. He had won the British

Middleweight Title in 1979, the year before Brian had commenced his professional career. Tony then went on to collect Commonwealth and European titles, before winning the right to meet one of boxing's all time greats, Marvin Hagler. In the fight before he met Brian, Sibson had made another unsuccessful attempt to win a World title, on which occasion he had lost to the durable, ageless Dennis Andries for the WBC and British light heavyweight titles.

Brian and Sibson met on 7 September with 'Sibbo's Commonwealth title and Brian's British title both on the line. Sibson took the fight in seven rounds and soon after Brian announced his retirement, expressing a wish to continue in the game as a referee. His decision to go out at the top was a wise one, especially with the likes of Nigel Benn, Chris Eubank and the tragic Michael Watson, starting to make an impression on the British and later World scenes.

HEROL GRAHAM

Freely spoken of as the greatest boxer never to win a world title, Nottingham born Herol 'Bomber' Graham was the boxer who revitalised boxing in South Yorkshire at the beginning of the 1980s.

He played a big part in making Sheffield a major boxing city and building a platform with his manager, Brendan Ingle, for a generation of fine fighters to build upon. Criticised in his early days for being too defensive and boring, Graham changed his style to become a knockout specialist and box office hit. After twice coming near to becoming a world champion, he campaigned after five years out of the ring for a licence and came within an ace of winning that elusive world crown, eighteen months short of his 40th birthday.

At eighteen it is arguable whether there was a better amateur boxer in Britain than Nottingham's Herol Graham. Boxing out of the Radford Club, he had reeled off National School titles in 1973, 1975 and 1976. He won the Junior ABA title in 1976, the NABC in 1976 and his last major title before turning professional, the 1978 ABA middleweight title. Herol was upset that the ABA win over Delroy Parkes didn't guarantee him automatic Commonwealth Games selection.

There wasn't long to reflect, for Sheffield trainer Brendan Ingle, had spotted his potential some time earlier and young Herol moved to Sheffield to begin his professional career, taking a room at Ingle's house. A natural southpaw, Brendan taught him to switch during a fight and confuse his opponent and helped his already classy defensive skills to such a level that his opponents found it almost impossible to even hit him. Brendan helped fuel the 'Bomber' Graham legend in the Sheffield area by touring round the Working Men's Clubs on a Sunday morning. Any punter who could land a punch could earn a fiver, though such were Herol's evasive abilities that a fiver never saw daylight from Brendan's pocket. When the modern boxing fan could no longer appreciate the skills of a defensive boxer and wanted knockouts in the Frank Bruno mould, Herol added aggression and punching abilities to his defensive skills.

In November 1978, at the age of nineteen, Herol made his

Herol 'Bomber' Graham, British and European Middleweight Champion, British, Commonwealth and European Light Middleweight Champion. *(Photo loaned by Bill Matthews).*

professional debut in Sheffield with a win over Vivian Waite. Before he was twenty-one, Graham had won his first fifteen fights, with over half of them coming in front of his fans in South Yorkshire. Quickly moving up the light middleweight ranks, 'Bomber' obtained a fight with the champion Pat Thomas at Sheffield in 1981. Welshman Thomas, before becoming British light middleweight champion, had twice won the British welterweight title and in his last light middleweight defence had won the Lonsdale Belt outright. Herol wasn't going to waste his chance in front of the Sheffield faithful. It was cautious safety first tactics from Herol who refused to open up. Thomas became further and further dispirited as he couldn't hit 'Bomber'. Unexciting to watch, it was clinically effective as Herol took the fight the full fifteen rounds to gain his first British title.

Huddersfield based boxer Prince Rodney had been in the top half dozen light middles for the last couple of years, so there was some surprise when the British Boxing Board of Control, failed to sanction Rodney's fight with Herol as a voluntary fight for the champion. It was a chance for Herol to silence the critics of his Thomas fight and 'Bomber' duly put Prince Rodney away in one round, felling him three times and even impressing the ringside Boy Green who was in the audience. Green twice fought unsuccessfully for the world welterweight title in 1977 and 1981.

The next action for Herol was a tilt at the Commonwealth light middleweight title against the holder, the cagey counter puncher, Kenny Bristol from Guyana. Bristol had been champion since 1979 and in a career that had started in 1976 he had only lost three times. In front of his own crowd Graham went fifteen rounds for a second time to win his second title. Both titles were on the line when he fought the modern day 'Cinderella Man' Chris Christian. The Stoke Newington man was easily outgunned and for the first time a 'Bomber' title fight had finished inside the distance. Impressive in an earlier Liverpool appearance when he stopped American, Larry Mayes, in four rounds, Herol returned for his third fight in front of one of the country's acknowledged crowds to outclass French African Fred Coranson.

While Herol had been cleaning up in the light middles, his stablemate Brian Anderson had been doing exactly the same and there was speculation whether the two mates would meet in the ring. Brendan Ingle confessed he would love to sit back and enjoy it and as 1982 ended, Anderson was rated number one challenger for Herol's titles by *Boxing News*.

For his first fight in 1982, Herol took his unbeaten record out of England for the first time, travelling to Lagos to defend his Commonwealth title against Hunter Clay, one of a number of young Nigerians considered to be potential world champions. It was a risky business fighting in Africa, not many fighters came home victorious and there was the heat and a patriotic crowd to think about. Herol added to his reputation with a fifteen round points win and his record stood at twenty-two wins with sixteen of them coming on points verdicts. The effect of his change of style from that of a defence based points winner to an aggressive, attacking, winning inside the distance world title contender, can be shown by the fact that in his next sixteen fights before he lost his unbeaten record, only one of those sixteen went the distance.

After a five round win over Tony Nelson at Wembley, Herol had his chance to fight for the vacant European light middleweight title which the Italian, Luigi Michillo had surrendered. His opponent was the wily veteran Luxembourg based Clemente Tshinza. Ten years as a professional, Tshinza had a fine record against British boxers, having won ten out of the eleven fights he had with British boxers, with the only man to beat him being Colin Jones, the world welterweight challenger; and even that result was due to a cut eye. Graham holding sixth ranking in the WBC ratings was the strong favourite, but there was a surprise when his opponent didn't last five minutes. 'Bomber' proving he did have a killer punch, finished the job off in one minute and forty-seven seconds of round two. As a result of a link-up with the Mike Barratt and Mickey Duff promotion team, there was now every likelihood of a world title fight in the none too distant future.

Carlos Betancourt fell in one round in Herol's next outing, this being followed by a trip to France to defend his new title. Thirty-six-year old Frenchman, Germaine Le Maitre was on the come-back trail, dominating the French light middleweight scene in the early 1970s. Le Maitre had retired in 1975 and returned in 1981 with three emphatic victories. Herol devastated the Frenchman with an eighth round barrage of blows, forcing the referee to stop the fight. Herol's crunching right had split Le Maitre's left eye and 4,000 French fans took it out on the referee, after he had called a doctor into the ring to end the affair. Stopped for the first time in thirteen years, the Frenchman announced his second retirement and related he had been beaten by a 'spider with long arms'. The French contest was his last as a light middle, for it had been thought for some time that he was ready to move into the much more attractive middleweight division.

Five inside the distance wins, none of them lasting longer than five rounds, including a three round stoppage of Leeds based Irish light heavyweight champion, Liam Coleman announced Herol's middleweight arrival.

In his 32nd fight Graham was matched with Jimmy Price for the vacant British middleweight title. Price had won fourteen of his fifteen fights and his only set-back had been against the former world light middleweight champion, Ayub Kalule. There was classic pre-match banter between Ingle and Price's manager Frank Warren. Frank accused 'Bomber' of having all his opponents handpicked, whilst Brendan, who was hoping matters would lead to a fight with WBC champion Marvin Hagler (four years champ, now nearing thirty), insisted that the problem was that not one of the rated fighters wanted to fight his man. The crowd had only just taken their seats and blinked and the fight was over, Herol destroying his fellow southpaw opponent in ninety seconds.

Barney Eastwood, the Belfast bookmaker who had steered Barry McGuigan to world honours, convinced Herol he could do the same for him and a saddened Brendan Ingle reluctantly let his fighter be taken over by the Irishman, though Brendan stayed on as his trainer. Herol's first appearance in his new home didn't go as well as hoped. The capacity crowd at the Usher Hall in Belfast gave him a rapturous reception when he entered the ring, but what they saw was not vintage 'Bomber' Graham. It was an untidy frustrating contest and sections of the crowd were not at all impressed and boos rang out after Graham's American opponent Sanderline Williams took him the full ten rounds. Graham won on points, making it his thirty-fourth consecutive win in an unbeaten record now stretching back over seven years.

Herol returned to Sheffield to pursue his challenge for the European middleweight title and his opponent was one of his hardest to date. Ayub Kalule, born in Uganda, had boxed out of Copenhagen for ten years. A former light heavyweight champion, he had only lost to three men who were or became world champions, one of which was Sugar Ray Leonard. Once again Graham had suffered difficulty in getting fights. His British rivals, Errol Christie and Mark Kaylor, had pulled out when nominated to fight him and even Kalule's manager Mogens Palle had tried hard to avoid the confrontation with the number one challenger for his man's title.

The Sheffield crowd went wild with delight as Graham stopped Ayub in ten rounds with a brilliant and powerful display of boxing. Kalule was, as expected, a hard opponent and Graham, despite being bloodied with cuts, had won eight of his nine fights as a middleweight on stoppages, and with Kalule a world rated boxer out of his way, the gate was now open for Herol's new manager to get him the world title fight he craved and deserved.

Eastwood took him to *Caesar's Palace*, Las Vegas for his first USA engagement, after getting Herol a fight on the Barry McGuigan versus Steve Cruz undercard. Though Barney returned home upset, his man McGuigan having surprisingly lost his world title in the desert heat, the one consolation was that 'Bomber' had won his contest in only ninety seconds. Herol's left hook took out Ernie Robotte much too soon for the American fight fans to get any impression of the true range and scope of the 'Bomber's' skill.

The never say die, full of determination, West Ham middleweight, Mark Kaylor, who had won fights by getting up off the floor, took on Graham in front of his own crowd at Wembley for 'Bomber's' European title. It was thought that if Graham could make the openings, he would overwhelm Mark with his punches and that was how it went. Kaylor received a cut eye from a clash of heads and couldn't stop Herol taking advantage of the injury. The brave Kaylor took considerable punishment, to the point where even he couldn't get off his stool to start the ninth round.

Tony Sibson, who had held the same European title twice in the past, lost to Marvin Hagler in a world title fight, and along with 'Bomber', the best British 'middle' of the late 1980s era, had failed to stop Kaylor in his points win over the West Ham man when he was champion. Dismissing Herol as a 'Limbo Dancer', Sibson elected to try his hand as a light heavyweight, but when he returned to the middleweight division it was Herol's stablemate Brian Anderson, he fought.

'Bomber' returned to Belfast for a seven round win over Charlie Boston, before his next fight, a second defence of his European title at Wembley against another European based African, Sumbu Kalambay.

His next fight following the defence was to be a world title fight for the vacant WBA title. He had been number one challenger to Iran Barkley and the Kalambay fight was seen as a warm up. Kalambay, whose record was thirty-seven wins out of forty-seven, was thought to be on the downward slope at the end of his career, but that proved totally incorrect, for the Italian/African had done his homework. Displaying all the usual Herol Graham attributes, and being just as slippery and difficult, Kalambay outgunned the champion. Kalambay took the European title on a twelve round points win and Herol's world title dream, for the moment, was off the agenda. There was one point of difference between this and Herol's other fights and that one point had a strong bearing on the result. For the first time Brendan Ingle wasn't in his corner, all the training had been done in Ireland supervised by Barney Eastwood and for the first time, Herol had lost.

While Kalambay took 'Bomber's' chance and won the WBA title, it was six months before the Herol Graham career was resumed, breaking himself back in with an eighth round stoppage over Ricky Stackhouse at Doncaster. By now the British middleweight scene was at its strongest with the arrival of Nigel Benn, Chris Eubank and Michael Watson. 'Bomber's' next fight in his comeback series was in a challenge for the British title vacated by Tony Sibson. Herol's opponent was one of his former sparring partners, James Crook. Eastwood was so sure of his man's success he wanted a £200,000 sidestake bet. Crook went in five rounds at Sheffield and Graham who had now won his Lonsdale Belt outright, wanted a rematch with the one man who had denied him his world title shot.

While talk was still going on about a return with Kalambay in Italy, Herol kept busy with a defence of his British title. Johnny Melfah, only two years as a professional and with only ten fights under his belt (thirty-four rounds in the ring against 'Bomber's' 272), shouldn't have been in the same championship ring as Graham. The 27-year-old Gloucester man who had started in the fairground booths was finished in five one-sided and hopeless rounds.

Three years older than Herol was Mike McCallum, who had been the WBA light middleweight champion from 1984 to 1987. Unbeaten he had relinquished the title to try his hand as a middleweight and it was a major surprise, as it had been when the Italian from Zaire beat Graham, when Kalambay beat him in a WBA title fight. When Kalambay was forced to give up his belt for not meeting 'Bomber', McCallum met the Sheffield based boxer instead at the Royal Albert Hall in front of 6,000 fans. The winner was due to meet the victor of the Nigel Benn versus Michael Watson fight.

Despite his talent, the Jamaican born McCallum (nicknamed the 'body snatcher') was never able to break into the big four ('Marvin Hagler, Roberto Duran, Thomas Hearns and Sugar Ray Leonard), money-go-round. He had one of boxing's legendary trainers in his corner in 77-year-old Eddie Futch. The old timer had Herol down for a hit and run merchant who didn't like to mix it. No fighter or not, 'Bomber' came within a whisker of beating his man. In a technically gruelling fight, McCallum jabbed his way to a split decision. A point deducted for swinging his opponent round cost Herol dear for the three judges' cards were 117 to 114 to Graham, 117 to 115 and 115 to 114 to McCallum. The Jamaican went on to beat Watson and Steve Collins, eventually moving up to light heavyweight and putting his name among the greats by winning three titles at different weights.

There had been a bust up with Eastwood over the McCallum fight and Graham didn't want him in his corner any more. Blaming Eastwood for the defeat, for with Brendan also in his corner giving one set of advice and Eastwood in the other giving different instructions, Herol's ears were full of contradictory advice. As it was, Eastwood was in hospital when Graham, in his first fight since the ill-fated world title fight, met Londoner Rod Douglas in a British middleweight title defence.

Douglas, a Commonwealth Games gold medallist in 1986 and unbeaten in fourteen fights, found it difficult to hit Graham who gradually wore his challenge down. The referee ended it in the ninth, when Douglas went down twice, despite protests from Mickey Duff, Douglas' manager who argued his man had been hit with the open glove.

After the Douglas fight Herol was inactive for a year before he was rewarded with another world title fight in 1990.

This time the WBC title was vacant (Roberto Duran had relinquished) and the fight was taken to a cabaret lounge of a casino in Marbella on the Costa Del Sol. Virgin Islander, Julian Jackson, had taken McCallum's old WBC light middle title and had been inactive due to a detached retina before he moved into the middleweight section and was matched with 'Bomber' for the vacant title. Jackson was a feared puncher. In forty fights he had won thirty-eight inside the distance, with thirty-three of his short wins on the trot. Herol produced three rounds of immaculate ringcraft. Jackson was bruised and bewildered. His eye was closed and 'Bomber' was boxing his head off, hitting him at will. The fight was there for the taking when Herol fell for the sucker punch in round four. Cornered by Graham, Jackson switched to southpaw, saw his opening and threw one of the most dramatic one punch finishes in boxing history. Graham fell to the ground, out before he hit the canvas. Knocked out for the first time in his career, Herol remained unconscious for several minutes. Perky afterwards, he talked of a lucky punch and a rematch. All he needed to do was lay off and box his usual tactics, for the referee revealed later he had decided because of his eye injury only to give Jackson one more round. Jackson kept his title for three years before losing it to Gerard McLellan.

It was another year before the Herol Graham career resumed, when in an ordered defence of his British title he met the top challenger, Alfreton's John Ashton. The fight had been put back after 30-year-old, Ashton needed a couple of months to recover from a cut eye received in an unsuccessful challenge for Sumbu Kalambay's European title. The fight saw Herol boxing in Sheffield after a three year gap in a Matchroom promotion at the City Hall. 'Bomber' had too much guile and experience for Ashton. The fight wasn't a classic, Graham was always the master and won in six rounds.

Nearly five years after they first met, Herol now got his rematch with Kalambay. It had been thought at thirty-one, he was over the hill and Sumbu had proved the doubters wrong by winning a world title. Now at thirty-six he was still European champion, and with 'Bomber' the challenger for his title he had to travel to the boxer's graveyard of Italy with his new manager Mickey Duff. Herol had been really hurt in their first encounter. More than in any other fight Herol was completing an act of revenge and he certainly looked on with great satisfaction when Kalambay took two early counts. However, the Sheffield man failed to press home his advantage and later on in the fight he fell foul of the referee who penalised him for spinning his opponent and hitting from behind. It was always going to be hard to get a verdict in Italy and Kalambay, who looked fitter in the second contest than he did in the first five years earlier, proved he was 'Bomber's' bogey, when he took the points verdict.

This second Kalambay defeat knocked on the head the chances of a third world title fight and at nearly thirty-three, the press speculated whether or not the 'Bomber's' retirement was imminent. It became a reality when on a double bill at Elland Road, which featured Henry Wharton versus 'Fidel Castro', Graham was stopped by the Manchester based, Bradford born fighter, Frank Grant. Limited as a boxer, Grant who carried the nickname 'The Hi-tech Terminator', had qualities of extreme fitness and carried a dangerous punch in either hand and his preparation by manager Phil Martin had included extensive sparring with southpaws. The fight exploded in round nine when Graham looked as if he was going for glory. Grant retaliated and trapped Herol on the ropes. Seizing his chance Grant put enough punches together to stop Herol and take away his title and send him into retirement, achieving lasting fame as the only British boxer to beat the 'Bomber'.

Obviously influenced by the likes of George Foreman who had defied time and returned after a lengthy absence to take a world title, seeing fighters winning versions of the numerous world titles that were available, some of whom were not fit to lace his boxing boots, plus the sense of under-achievement with one big ambition to fulfil, saw Herol decide he wanted to box again. For a while a licence proved a difficulty but, after four years out of the game, Herol began his comeback in Sheffield.

American Terry Ford, nine pounds lighter, was his opponent. An extensive series of gym sessions paid off for, despite his timing being out on occasions, Herol completed his comeback with an eight round points win.

Following the same distance win over Bradford's Craig Joseph, 37-year-old Graham had his first big test when he met Chris Johnson for the vacant WBC international super middleweight title at Olympia. Graham was the 6-1 underdog against the unbeaten Canadian, who was considered future championship material. Herol put himself back on the world's stage when he rocked Johnson in the fourth and could afford a couple of grins for he recognised the inevitable as Johnson was finished in the eighth after being floored the previous round. A twelve round points win over Vinny Pazienza in his title defence and in only four comeback fights, Herol had the chance to make history.

Self-managed, Herol linked up with Lennox Lewis' manager, Frank Maloney and challenged Charles 'The Hatchet' Brewer, the IBF super middleweight champion in Atlantic City, on the undercard of Lewis' WBC heavyweight defence against Shannon Briggs. No boxer as old as thirty-eight had ever won a world title for the first time and despite the obvious disadvantages, Herol was always in with a shout for it was known that Brewer hated southpaws and counter-punchers. For a third time it became a case of so near and yet so far. Herol floored Brewer twice with left hand shots in the third round and was ahead on at least one judge's card, when 'Father Time' caught up with him towards the end and his legs went. One minute he was in contention, the next Brewer had taken over. The fight was terminated in the tenth and afterwards even tough promoter Maloney joined in the dressing-room tears. The short comeback had ended at the top and though Herol joined a list of fighters, the likes of Tony Sibson, Henry Wharton and Alan Rudkin who made three unsuccessful world title attempts, to become one of boxing's nearly men, it is very doubtful if anyone could have come closer.

JOHNNY NELSON

s 1999 ended and the new millenium arrived in South
Yorkshire, it is hard to think of a more popular sportsman
and ambassador for Sheffield than Johnny Nelson.
Despite not having the best of starts to his professional career and
becoming a figure of ridicule and abuse, after two lack-lustre world
title fights in the early 1990s, so much so that he had to fight
successfully all over the world to regain the respect of his home town
crowd, before returning in triumph with five world title wins during
the last year of the twentieth century and even had his name
discussed as a potential opponent for heavyweight legend, Mike
Tyson in the first year of the 21st century.

It was Johnny's brother Alan who had the initial interest in boxing
as a kid. Johnny was more often spoken of in connection with his
prowess at basketball and sprinting. Eventually, when he was about
fourteen, he followed Alan down to Brendan Ingle's gym and the
Irish master did not at first realise the two boys were brothers, until
he called at the Nelson home to sign Alan as a professional. Big
Johnny didn't break any pots as an amateur, but Brendan must have
seen something in him. Nonetheless it was a surprise in the gym
when he gave Johnny his professional ticket. The doubters looked to
be right when Johnny lost his first three professional fights on points
during 1986. However, Nelson dug in and won his next four, the
seventh fight being the first time he had stopped an opponent, when
the referee stepped in to prevent further punishment to Sean Daley
in round one at Manchester. Following the initiative taken in
America, in the same year Johnny had turned professional, Britain
introduced a cruiserweight division (190 lb). The new weight, in
between light heavy and heavyweight, really became a necessity due
to the increased weight of the modern heavyweights. Boxing as a
cruiser and working in Brendan's gym with the likes of Herol
Graham, who became a great mate, Johnny even moved into a room
in 'Bomber's' flat. The opportunity to work out with a boxer of
'Bomber's' class brought him on by leaps and bounds, helping him
to develop excellent defensive techniques and, as a result, making
him an awkward opponent for a lot of fighters.

Johnny Nelson, Sheffield's World Cruiserweight Champion.

His record improved to twelve wins out of seventeen fights including nine wins from his last ten outings. One of his best wins was against the up and coming Crawford Ashley from Leeds, and Johnny visualised that Ashley would be one of his great rivals. But Crawford elected to box in the light heavyweight division and won British, European and Commonwealth titles at that weight.

Andy Straughn, who had become the second ever holder of the British cruiserweight title in 1986, was champion again and Johnny, who had won his first title, a Central Area crown, after a two round win over Danny Lawford, was matched against a very reluctant champion. The 29-year-old Barbados born left-hander, who had an immaculate amateur record (three successive ABA titles from 1979 to 1980 and an appearance in the Moscow Olympics), did not like Johnny's awkward style and considered the Sheffield man too slippery and an all round difficult proposition. The fight had been arranged by Straughn's former manager, Burt McCarthy, but the champion, who was now self-managed, was more interested in fighting for a European title.

Twenty-two-year-old Nelson had arranged for time off work from his job at Constant Security, to travel to London where he appeared on the Nigel Benn versus Michael Watson bill, fought in front of a 7,000 Finsbury Park crowd. The Hitchin based Straughn's fears were confirmed and Johnny knocked him out in eight rounds. Brendan, overjoyed to gain another British champion, thought he could have finished it in the third round.

The championship was a tonic for Herol Graham, still getting over his recent world title defeat against Mike McCallum. An over-the-moon 'Bomber', couldn't believe his lodger and sparring partner had come so far, he had always joked that Johnny was rubbish.

After a break for a holiday with 'Bomber', Johnny was ready for his first title defence. His opponent was 24-year-old Bolsover miner Ian Bulloch, who had lost two out of fourteen contests and beaten Dave Garside in an official title eliminator. Bulloch had beaten Johnny as an amateur and was confident in front of his own boisterous supporters at Victoria Hall, Hanley. The fight only lasted four minutes fifty-five seconds. Johnny's vicious right and left combination silenced the group of excessively noisy and potentially intimidating miners. The perfect execution of the combination saw Bulloch fall pole-axed to the canvas. With tensions high, there was the expected brawling outside the ring, with the police moving in quickly to arrest the ringleaders.

In early 1990 England could boast its own World cruiserweight champion when Glen McCrory, a guy with film star looks from the north-east, had won the IBF championship. There was talk of a match with Nelson, but McCrory, who had been undefeated British champion before seeking world honours, didn't fancy meeting Johnny Nelson, having his eye on more lucrative fights with American opponents.

It was after a three fight deal with Barry Hearn was signed that Johnny got to fight Puerto Rican, Carlos De Leon for the more fashionable WBC title. Leon, twelve years older at thirty-five, had won the title in 1982 after fifteen gruelling rounds with Marvin Camel and was now in his fourth spell as WBC champion. He had fought Evander Holyfield, who held both other versions, in a unification bout and had been blown away, though he didn't go down. His recent victory was against Johnny Reeson, the former British and European title holder. Leon's record prior to the fight read forty-four wins out of forty-nine matches. According to the bookies Nelson was 16-1 to win by a knockout and 40-1 for it to happen in the fight's early stages. Nelson was pleased to be boxing in front of his own Sheffield fans, though by the end of the contest, most of his supporters weren't too pleased with him. The fight ended in a doleful draw with Leon retaining his title, but what angered onlookers was that what was supposed to have been a world title fight, was in fact more like a sparring contest with very few real punches coming from either man. Fans, some of whom had paid £100 for ringside seats, walked out over a big fight that never was.

Johnny, who froze as the occasion got to him, was later to apologise and rather tongue in cheek admit that he himself fell asleep watching the video of the fight.

Resuming his fight career three months later with a seven round win over Dino Homsey in Brentwood, it would be six years before Johnny Nelson would box in Sheffield again. Building worker Lou Gent was the next challenger for Johnny's British title. Gent's manager, Greg Steene, reported that his man, who had an up and down career winning sixteen out of twenty-two was at his fittest ever and would make the most of his second chance at the title. He had previously lost to McCrory. A vicious uppercut by Nelson in round four ended with Johnny winning his Lonsdale Belt outright.

Two fights later, a fortnight before Christmas 1990, Johnny had his first fight in Germany when he fought for the vacant European title. Carrying an unbeaten record of just short of three years into the fight, Johnny was ahead on all three judges' cards, when he knocked out German champion Markus Bott with twelve seconds to go in the

Johnny Nelson

LONSDALE

In his corner

twelfth and final round. Once again it had been the trademark Nelson uppercut that had done the trick.

The experienced 29-year-old Belgian, Yves Monsieur, who had been the distance with two world champions, was expected to give Johnny a hard test in his first European defence. The affair produced eight one-sided rounds and when Johnny took heed of his corner's demand to step up his work rate, the Belgian cornerman threw in the towel.

The Monsieur fight was his only fight during 1991 and after various other planned fights had fallen through for one reason or another (Johnny had relinquished his British title), the next occasion Johnny Nelson entered the ring was for another crack at the world title. The date was May 1992, the venue Fredericksburg, USA and his opponent was one of the fight games great characters James Warring, the IBF champion. Warring had had a very colourful career. Aged thirty-three he had only fought twenty times winning eighteen and drawing one. He'd been a kick boxer and part-time actor and had won his world title in Italy in only twenty-four seconds, the fifth shortest title fight ever, when he beat James Pritchard. Sadly the fight was similar to the first time Nelson had fought for a world title. Ingle blamed the fighter's tenseness but still backed his man to come back and become a champion. Johnny, in a dismal points loss, failed to throw enough punches or show any aggression and certainly didn't look like the man who had flattened Bott. His range was out with the fourteen month lay off and this was one of the key factors contributing to his failure against Warring.

The effect of the Warring fight was very apparent in his next two outings, when he suffered two more defeats, in one of which, his 29th contest, he was stopped for the first time in his professional career.

No longer a draw in England, Johnny, whose last three fights had been in the USA, France and South Africa, travelled to Melbourne for his next contest, a challenge for the WBF cruiserweight title. His opponent was naturalised Australian, Dave Russell, who had been born in Newcastle. Brendan, with one of his fighters at an engagement in Berlin, couldn't make the trip and missed his man at the third time of trying to win a version of the world title, although it wasn't under the auspices of a boxing body recognised by the British Boxing Board of Control.

The fight was terminated in the eleventh round with a technical knockout. Nelson was impressive, with business-like counter-punching and unerring accuracy. After the fight, Russell announced his retirement.

In a rare British appearance at Mansfield in Nottinghamshire, he met Tom Collins, the Leeds based light heavyweight who had collected the British title on three occasions during the 1980s, in his first defence of his new title. Collins at thirty-eight was on his last hurrah and though he'd been in the ring with some good men, he had lost more than twenty fights. Johnny took the chance to put his name back in favour in England in a one round exhibition of ruthless boxing. Collins looked out of shape and went down three times inside three minutes, giving referee John Coyle no alternative but to call a halt to the one-sided contest. Thus Johnny sent a second boxer in succession into retirement.

Nelson lost his title in his second defence when he was beaten on a disqualification in a contest in Belgium against Frances Wanyama. The affair ended in round ten when, after an early warning for holding and pushing, the referee sent Johnny back to his dressing-room. Brendan moaned that both boxers had been as bad as one another and the annoying thing was that Johnny was ahead on two of the judges cards' when he was sent out of the ring.

Australia, remembering him from his fight with Russell, was keen to get Nelson out there to tackle Johnny Thunder, the WBF heavyweight champion. At first the fight looked as if it would take place in Melbourne, but eventually took place in Auckland, New Zealand where Johnny conceded 22lb to his opponent. Thunder tried a round of big bombs and his lack of accuracy cost him his title. Johnny's use of the ring and ropes coupled with his constant movement and effective left jab gave him yet another title.

His success as a heavyweight saw Johnny meet the European and Commonwealth heavyweight champion Henry Akinwande in a ten round non-title fight. Henry hadn't lost once in his twenty-four fights and had beaten 'Thunder', for his Commonwealth title. Akinwande had been down to fight American veteran James 'Bonecrusher' Smith who had failed a medical. Brendan, always quick to see an opportunity, came to promoter Duff's rescue by letting Johnny take the fight at very short notice. The 6ft 7in world ranked Akinwande (five inches taller than Nelson), entered the ring two stones heavier than Johnny's 14st 10lb. Ingle answered criticism of his fighter as a negative spoiler, by telling everyone his man had done a better job on 'Thunder' than Henry had. Despite Akinwande's physical advantages, he could not put the Sheffield man away, though he had done enough to beat Johnny on points. Akinwande would go on to compete successfully in America, win the WBO title and only later lose his first fight to Lennox Lewis in a challenge for the WBC title.

The next two stops on the Johnny Nelson world tour were Thailand and Sao Paulo, Brazil. He outpointed Nicolai Kulpin of Kazakhstan in the Thai tourist town of Chiang Rai. It was a closely fought match and Johnny won a split decision. He was 35lb lighter and was able to dance around his slow, cumbersome opponent, but couldn't raise the power to finish him off. Willing to fight anywhere, Johnny's travels took him to Sao Paulo to meet Adilson Rodriques. Here, Johnny said goodbye to his heavyweight title in a twelve round points defeat and lost again when he returned three months later to Brazil as Rodriques' challenger. It looked as if Johnny was out to beat some record for the number of countries he had fought in, when he had a fight arranged in Saint Petersburg, Russia against their cruiser champion Serguai Corolav. The trip was eventually cancelled at the eleventh hour when the Russian cried off with injury.

His world travels over for the moment, Johnny beat fellow Yorkshireman Tony Booth in two rounds and then finally fought in Sheffield again, where he faced another British legend, Dennis Andries in an attempt to regain his old British cruiserweight title. The records showed Dennis as being forty-three years old, but it was widely believed he was nearer fifty. It had been six years since he had been stopped in the ring by Jeff Harding but it was obvious the old warhorse's days were numbered when the referee sent him back to his corner fifty-three seconds into the seventh round, pronouncing Johnny the victor.

As well as winning his British cruiserweight crown back, Johnny also regained the European title, when he overwhelmed Patrice Aouissi in round seven in France. Johnny had actually been in France sparring with Aouissi, helping the Frenchman prepare to fight Terry Dunstan for the vacant title, when Dunstan pulled out only a few days before the fight. Johnny took the late substitute role. Aouissi thought he had nothing to beat, but the wily fox Nelson hadn't shown all of his repertoire.

Johnny ended 1997 with a forty-three second defence of his European title against Benelux champion Dirk Wallyn at Sheffield and Johnny was starting to win back respect from the city's acknowledged fight fans.

Johnny had a rival over the Pennines in the Frank Warren managed Carl Thompson. After losing in his first attempt, Thompson had taken the WBO cruiserweight title in October 1997. Chris Eubank's decision to move up to cruiserweight gave the division a considerable boost and there was a lot of interest in the eccentric Eubank's challenge for Thompson's world title. Thompson beat him and Nelson, sensing some big money matches, was wanting a slice of the action. Nelson's challenge was ignored for a return with Eubank which Thompson won. Johnny kept in trim with a six round win over Peter Oboh the London based Nigerian. Thompson had retired Eubank and Johnny became a number one contender for the WBO crown. Thompson seemed to be holding out for the best deal. Johnny's concentration on his effort to obtain a world title fight, saw him lose his European title for failing to meet Alexander Gurov of the Ukraine, when the date was set Johnny was suffering from a back injury.

1999 proved to be Johnny's greatest year in the sport. He won a recognised world title and he also won over the city's sports followers, being awarded a civic reception for his endeavours. The world title fight with the 34-year-old, Carl Thompson had been arranged for February, but the Manchester man had it delayed to March on the pretence he needed more preparation. There were plenty of verbal exchanges between the rivals in the press and Johnny, with a big chance at last and a point to prove, was simply too fast for Thompson and stopped him in five rounds. Thompson stayed away from the post-fight conference, but sent a message saying he wanted a rematch. With some of his old work mates from the security firm leading the applause, Johnny Nelson took the plaudits as a world champion and this time the title was recognised world-wide. Whilst there was talk of lucrative matches with the WBA champion Fabrice Tiozzo or the WBA holder Juan Carlos (Black Panther) Gomes, Johnny opted for a quick defence against Hackney based West Indian, Bruce Scott.

Despite his recent British and Commonwealth titles, Scott wasn't the big draw it was hoped and Johnny was guilty of trying too hard to please. Scott won applause for his gameness but barely won a round as Johnny completed his first defence on points.

A native American Indian from Alberta, Willard Lewis, unbeaten in fifteen fights, was Johnny's next challenger. Lewis wasn't in Nelson's class and after the contest ended, the American Indian needed eleven stitches. Fast cleaning up the cruiser division, there was more talk of Johnny becoming a permanent heavyweight.

Before the year was out there was time for two more defences.

Las Vegas was the scene for his meeting with little known 25-year-old Tongan, Sione Asipeli. The Tongan went down in round ten but survived to the end with Johnny a clear winner. His fight with Frenchman Christopher Gerard took place at the height of the beef war with France. Johnny made the point, British beef was best as he ended the most successful year of his career with five world title fights and five wins. As the new century arrived, there looked to be plenty more mileage on the Johnny Nelson clock.

PAUL JONES

Only two months after Prince Naseem Hamed had the honour of becoming Sheffield's first world champion, the city crowned a second champion when, in a career which had seen him retire two years before making a comeback, Paul 'Silky' Jones landed the WBO light middleweight title three days past his 29th birthday and not a year into his ring return. Jones' feat, made him the first boxer actually to win his crown fighting in Sheffield. Johnny Nelson won cruiser and heavyweight titles in 1993 under WBF rules. The WBF never received the same recognition as the four main bodies, WBA, WBC, IBF and WBO.

After becoming interested in boxing at Hillsborough Boys' Club, Paul Jones became another Brendan Ingle protégé at the age of twelve. The lovable Irishman sometimes had his hands full as Paul occasionally got into trouble. His worst offence was when he was charged with assault and received a six months' driving ban. Jones boxed for the Unity Amateur Club and though he often talked of emigrating to America where he had relatives, he took his professional ticket with Brendan. Commencing with points wins over Paul Gillings and Pat Durkin, his next two fights ended in defeats for Paul. In the second loss at Manchester where Humphrey Harrison beat him on points, the Sheffield lad was booed out of the ring for clowning and warned for ungentlemanly conduct. Jonesy announced that he wasn't bothered for he was 'heading out west'.

From late 1988 and through 1989 he boxed out of Toronto, Canada. In the seven fights he had there he won five and was beaten twice. When he heard that Paul had been disqualified in round six for biting against Donovan Boucher, Brendan was fuming. Paul was still a novice, he claimed, and the Sheffield manager was critical of the matching, for Boucher was Canadian welterweight champion and world ranked. Returning to England, with only two defeats in his next seven fights and most of the wins inside the distance, Paul earned a crack at Jason Rowe's light middleweight Central Area title. Ingle tipped his man as a future champion as he carried off an emphatic ten round points win over Leeds man Rowe to win his area title.

Training at Brendan's gym with the likes of Herol Graham, whom

Paul 'Silky' Jones, with two of his fans. *(photo by kind permission of B. Parkin).*

he accompanied to Spain as one of his sparring partners in his preparation for his world title fight, had made Paul Jones a good prospect and he ended 1990 with six defeats out of his total of twenty fights.

His only defeat in the next two years was in Spain where he lost in two rounds to Hugo Marinagelli. Then there came a shock defeat against Paul Wesley in November 1992 in front of a home town crowd in Doncaster. Jones was stopped in two rounds and Birmingham based Wesley had lost twenty out of thirty-eight fights. His record during 1991-1992 had read, fought twelve, won two. By the end of the century, Wesley had lost twice as many as he had won, but to be fair to Wesley he did show his durability by going the distance with the likes of Steve Collins, Chris Pyatt and Sumbu Kalambay and also went the distance when he did get a fight for the British title.

Disillusioned with the game, Paul Jones dropped out of the scene. Inactive during 1993-1994, Paul eventually returned to sparring in an attempt to alleviate money problems, before eventually making a decision to commence fighting again.

The come-back was with a different management and with his nickname 'Silky' more prominent in his publicity, Paul signed for Barry Hearn, the snooker manager, who was at that time making inroads into boxing with his Matchroom promotion and management team.

After helping Steve Collins in his preparation for his fight with Chris Eubank, 'Silky' beat Julian Eavis in four rounds at Worcester in his first come-back fight. A second win, this time over Peter Waudby, saw Jones put forward by Hearn as a challenger for the vacant WBO inter-continental light middleweight title. To fight for the title, Jonesy had to cross the sea to Belfast to take on Ulsterman, Damian Denny in his own backyard. An uppercut dropped Denny to the canvas and Paul returned home after an early round win, boasting his first major title. There was a return to Belfast for a quick defence where he recorded a points victory over the African, Danny Juma. The man from Ghana had a reputation for being dangerous, but Paul's jab kept him at long range and Juma couldn't break the Sheffield man's dominance. After the Juma win, Hearn promised his man he'd get him a world title fight.

New York born Verno Phillips had been the WBO world light middleweight champion until recently, losing his title to the 37-year-old Gianfranco Rosi and Hearn was confident his man would become Rosi's first challenger. After another sucessful defence of his inter-continental title against South African, Eric Spalding in two rounds, 'Silky' got his chance but not against Rosi. Phillips had taken his title back for Rosi, it was revealed, had failed a dope test.

The same week Naseem Hamed had won the WBO featherweight title, it was announced that 28-year-old Jones would fight Verno Phillips at Sheffield and 'Silky' was hopeful that Naz, who was a close friend, would be in attendance. Phillips had moved to South America in 1990 and had been unbeaten in ten fights there. Before the Rosi fight he had made three successful defences and also had a decision over the WBA champion, Julio Cesar Vasquez, which was clouded in controversy when a cornerman had interfered in the fight.

The fight, Sheffield's first World title fight, was promoted by local men Dennis Hobson and Peter Hayman, in a joint agreement with Tommy Gilmour. Experts were of the opinion that Phillips would be too good for the Sheffield man who in a year had come from the dole, to win five fights on his come-back trail and was now fighting for a world title in his home town. The fight went the distance and the result was a split points verdict in favour of the challenger. Jones, who had done all his pre-fight training down in Romford with the Matchroom boys, had only returned to Sheffield shortly before the fight and had his pals Naz, Herol Graham and Johnny Nelson cheering him on. The American, who complained about Paul butting, for which Jones received a warning, only waned in the last three rounds. Paul's work at the end, just edged it for him, for earlier in the fight he had kept a healthy distance from the champion. It was Phillips' first time out of America and now his career was in doubt.

Whilst Sheffield crowned another champion, no one could have realised that 'Silky' Jones would never defend his title and wouldn't have another fight for a year.

Hearn had plans for Paul to defend his title in America against Bronko McKart. There was a fall-out between manager and boxer, and, accused of failing to defend his title, the WBO stripped him. Jones maintained a hand injury had prevented him from taking the fight. Jones wanted to fight the decision with lawyers, pleading he had both a doctor's note and a specialist's confirmation. He related he had refused the initial purse, but had subsequently agreed a cash deal and it was while training for the fight that the injury had happened. With Jones in the cold, McKart beat unranked Puerto Rican Santos Cordana at Indian Springs.

There was a year left on his contract with Hearn and Paul told the press he wouldn't fight for Hearn again, preferring to go it alone.

In June 1996 'Silky' was in America training at the famous Kronk Gym in Detroit (the home of the legend Tommy 'Hitman' Hearns) with trainer Glyn Rhodes. There were management talks with Frank Maloney and there was talk of Paul meeting Ensley Bingham, who had won the British light middleweight title earlier in the year. That fight failed to materialise because Bingham took a fight for Jones' former world title with a new champion Ronald Wright, who had deposed fellow American and short-lived champion McKart.

Eventually the rift with Hearn was healed and 'Silky' returned to Romford to work under Freddie King.

Eager to be in action, he met a 'young pretender' in Ryan Rhodes, one of his old manager Brendan Ingle's star pupils. The pair had sparred when Rhodes was very young and learning the ropes. Ryan had won all his first ten fights and the match was for the British light middleweight title. Bingham had given up the title in a quest for higher honours. Rhodes had just gone twenty, and though he had only two years' experience as a professional, he had been attending Brendan's gym long before he was a teenager. Jones himself had just passed thirty. Sheffield was the natural venue and the two local men met at Ponds Forge.

Frank Warren was promoting the bout and he was really upset when 'Silky' failed to show up at the usual pre-fight press conference. He threatened to dock Jones' purse for a contract break. Jones was also in trouble, when he was twenty-five minutes late for the weigh-in. He weighed in three-quarters of a pound over and needed a sparring session to take off the weight. Young Rhodes took the honours and afterwards Paul had no complaints. 'I got beat and lost to a champion', he acknowledged. The eighth round stoppage caused him to consider another retirement, but he was soon back in training and in his next fight he stopped Lee Blundell in four rounds at Mansfield.

In October 1997 he was matched with South African, Johnson Tshuma, for the vacant Commonwealth middleweight title. The weight difficulty made him decide to compete as a full-blown middleweight. Jonesy nearly pulled off a dramatic win in the last round but finally lost the decision on points. His effort earned him a rematch and he proved he had learnt from the first encounter, when he beat Tshuma to take the title.

In his first defence of his new title, he met Hackney middleweight, Jason Matthews. A late starter, Matthews didn't have his first professional fight until he was twenty-five and had recently held the WBO inter-continental middleweight title. The clash for Jones' Commonwealth title was at Oldham and events at the fight would cause the Sheffield man to make another retirement decision.

Nicknamed 'The Method Man', Matthews entered the ring with a record of nineteen wins out of twenty. By now Paul was self-managed, under new trainer Maurice Corr, of Manchester. The fight ended in round seven when the 1,000 crowd erupted after the top of the bill fight had been stopped, with the referee disqualifying 'Silky' for persistent holding. In fact, he had already lost the title before the fight started, weighing in $3^1/_2$lb over the limit. A riot started and in an effort to avoid the mass brawling, a man had run out of the doors of the fight venue and had been killed by a passing motor coach.

At thirty-two, criticised for a poor display and in a career in which he had courted his own brand of controversy, Paul 'Silky' Jones announced his retirement. He stated he was a saddened man following the events at Oldham and, if that was the way the sport was going, he wanted no further part in it and had no wish to fight again.

However, the itching to box again returned in 2000 and Jones eased his way back in the sport competing in local promotions by Glyn Rhodes.

CHRIS SAUNDERS

It was unexpected in many quarters, but not to his manager, Brendan Ingle, who knew he could beat the seemingly invincible champion, Del Bryan. Christopher Saunders, who hadn't exactly set boxing alight, losing as many as he had won in his thirty or so fights, pulled off the big shock of 1995 when he proved to be the man who, at the third time that a boxer from Barnsley had tried for it, brought home to the town the British welterweight title. It was a staggering seventy-eight years after Charlie Hardcastle had won Barnsley its only other British title when he won the featherweight title in 1917.

Born in 1969, Chris, like many young boxers before him, was influenced by his father and it was that influence which made Hoyland youngster Christopher Saunders take up the noble sport. Barry Saunders, whose father had been an army champion, saw his son put through his early paces at Arthur O'Loughlin's gym in Wombwell. Chris reached the quarter-finals of the NBC tournaments but had no immediate plans for a ring career. He did a two year YTS scheme at Stocksbridge Steelworks before other jobs saw him become a furniture delivery man and a fork-lift truck driver. Still keeping his interest in boxing, he trained at Wombwell Baths under Derek Walker before taking the professional route in 1990, when he signed for manager Frank Maloney.

Saunders started with two points wins and then made it a hat-trick when he stopped Justin Graham in three rounds in his first Sheffield appearance. Form faded and he only won three of his next four fights before he met Billy Schwer, the Luton based boxer with a big Irish following. Schwer, who campaigned as a lightweight, had won all his first seven fights, the majority of them in the first round. Chris couldn't cope with Schwer's explosive punching and like earlier Schwer contests, the referee stopped the fight in the first round. Schwer had been the first man to stop the Barnsley welter inside the distance and to show the result wasn't a fluke, Schwer repeated the dose three Saunders' fights later. Chris, succumbed in the third round, the second time he had been stopped inside the distance. Schwer certainly was a tough cookie, Saunders' second defeat at his

At the third time of trying the British welterweight titles is won by Barnsley man, **Chris Saunders.**

hands was his eleventh straight win, with only one of his fights going past round three, and within eighteen months, he was British and Commonwealth lightweight champion.

In his eighteenth fight, Chris challenged for his first title when he lost a Central Area light welterweight challenge on points in Liverpool against Richard Burton. Prospects after that did not look good, for Saunders didn't win any of his next five fights and was getting to the stage where his record was showing that he had lost more fights than he had won. From February 1992 to December 1993, he fought nine times, losing seven and drawing one.

Among those defeats was a match where he met another champion in the making on his way to the top, Scouser, Shea Neary, who prior to meeting Chris had won his first three fights inside the distance. Chris proved he had the staying power to take him the full course and Neary was to prove his class with an unbeaten run which would take him to the WBU welter title.

Ending 1993 with sixteen defeats out of twenty-six contests, 1994 was the year when everything would change for Chris Saunders. Finally believing in himself, he was to put a seven fight winning sequence together which would climax with a British championship.

He made a good start to the year when he ended Kevin Lueshing's unbeaten record. The Beckenham man had won all his eleven fights bar one, inside the distance and Saunders with his dismal record was considered an easy oppenent and was fully expected by the boxing press to become victim number twelve. In his most impressive fight so far, he stunned Lueshing, who had beaten the legendary Kirkland Laing who had a decision over another even bigger legend Roberto Duran, in a Southern Area light middleweight fight. In his last outing, the referee stopped the Ebbw Vale contest in four rounds. Chris Saunders had started to turn the corner.

In Chris' first trip abroad, a two round knockout of Jose Varela, the former European welterweight champion, another man with a reputation as a knockout specialist, in his own country of Germany,was another career booster. Three wins in two months in local promotions against Julian Eavis, whom he beat twice and Lindon Scarlett who had a month earlier gone twelve rounds in an unsuccessful challenge for Del Bryan's British welterweight title, was followed up by a second win in Europe where he stopped the Swede, Roberto Welin a former amateur champion who at one time had been guided by Angelo Dundee whom he stopped in seven rounds in Italy, brought to a close a very successful year.

Since Maloney, he had been with Ken Richardson of Retford for a spell, but now in Brendan Ingle's hands, Saunders had a new ring of confidence. Brendan had spoken several times of the fact that in his opinion, his man could beat Delroy Bryan. Del had been champion on and off since 1991, when he beat Kirkland Laing for the title and by the time Chris got to meet him in September 1995, Delroy, since regaining the title in 1993, had made three successful defences.

There was a big disappointment that the fight couldn't be held in Barnsley. The new Metrodome was freely talked about, but the lack of a major sponsor saw the fight go to Mansfield Leisure Centre, under a Frank Warren and Alma Ingle promotion. Sky TV pundits, Barry McGuigan and Duke McKenzie both tipped Bryan, whom they talked of as being in world class, to make a fourth successful defence. The 28-year-old Nottingham born, Birmingham based champion's record stood at forty-five fights, thirty-two wins, one draw and twelve defeats.

There was a sensational opening round when Saunders dumped Bryan on the seat of his pants midway through the first round with a right cross. Bryan recovered and by the middle of the fight had got back on top. The champion was always the better boxer but Saunders still had a puncher's chance and in the eighth round the fight changed direction again when Bryan was felled a second time but once again he recovered to get back into the fight. However, Saunders couldn't be denied and he came again

at the end of the eleventh round. In the last round the champion was reeling from two further knockdowns. At the end of the round, Barnsley had finally won its welterweight title and Ingle who had masterminded his rise from boxing obscurity, retorted that Chris deserved it, showing guts, power and a never-say-die attitude in a brilliant performance.

A three times a day, seven days a week training regime had paid dividends. Bryan's career slumped after the defeat and he ended 1998 with six successive defeats including two against another Yorkshireman, Sheffield's Ryan Rhodes, another great Brendan Ingle prospect.

Having won every fight since his only defeat by Saunders, Kevin Lueshing earned his right to challenge for Chris' title, when he stopped Michael Smyth in three rounds at Cardiff in an official eliminator and the pair met five months after the Barnsley man's title win, the venue for the defence being in London. The fight was scheduled for the London Docklands Arena, but on the day before the fight, the capital was rocked by a bomb blast. The Barnsley fight contingent were only 100 yards from the blast. The event was put back a couple of days and Chris returned to London to a new venue, the York Hall, Bethnal Green.

Lueshing had something to prove and what followed was seven

Chris in training with 'Naz'.

minutes of brutal boxing which contained seven separate knock downs. With Saunders down five times and the challenger twice, the fight was stopped sixty-two seconds into the third round when the referee decided he had seen enough. Chris' defence had been non-existent and Lueshing was the new champion. Chris blamed the bomb blast and the delay afterwards for his lack of concentration and with the score between the new champion and Chris standing at one each, Ingle expected his man to get a decider. Lueshing went on to try his hand on a bigger stage and, after winning the vacant IBO welter title in America, he lost in three rounds to Felix Trinidad in Nashville in a losing challenge for the IBF welterweight title.

Like Bryan after his title loss, Saunders failed to stay in title contention. Two defeats by Irishman Michael Carruih and lost eliminators against Scott Dixon in Glasgow and Derek 'The Rebel' Roche, the Irishman based in Leeds and on his way in an unbeaten run to the title, put him further behind in the welterweight stakes and as the new century arrived another crack at the title for the brave Barnsley boxer seemed remote.

PRINCE NASEEM HAMED

When Herol Graham dropped out of the spotlight in 1992 Sheffield, and not long after, all Britain had another hero to worship. With an unbeaten run into the new century, South Yorkshire's self-styled fighting machine, Prince Naseem Hamed, was well on the way to becoming what he had always dreamed of being, a worldwide boxing legend.

For all his flamboyance and at times exaggerated arrogance which sometimes may upset people but always fills boxing stadiums, there is one fact that cannot be denied about Naseem Hamed and that is his boxing talent. An array of perfected styles, among which he can switch and adapt during a fight, often make him an impossible target for his opponent to hit. But most of all an ability to destroy a man with awesome and at times unbelievable punching power, has firmly planted him in a place of honour on the world boxing stage.

Naseem Hamed was born in Sheffield in 1974. His Yemini father, Saleem, had arrived in England by boat in 1958 and was followed by his wife four years later. Sal worked in a steel mill in Sheffield and put his savings into a shop which was near Brendan Ingle's gym in Wincobank. Naseem was the fifth of his eight children and his third son. His father's concern for the racial abuse his sons had to bear was behind their first appearances at Brendan's gym. But before this arrival, the Irishman had spotted young Naseem getting the better of three older boys whilst travelling on a bus in his locality. Even before he was ten, Naseem had a brazen and cocky attitude and by the time he had reached his early teens, Ingle had been convinced for some time that he had a future champion on his hands.

'Bomber' Graham was Naseem's obvious idol, and so keen was Ingle to show

him off to the Sheffield public that he obtained permission to include him in a show at the Cutler Hall when he was still twelve. His opponent had a punching reputation, but young Naz tied him in knots. At thirteen he won his first national schools' title and boys' club and junior ABA titles at flyweight soon followed. Hamed captained Young England against America, at seventeen and in all lost only five out of his sixty-seven amateur contests. His five defeats were all controversial and already he was upsetting amateur officialdom with his lack of respect for opponents and his over-the-top ring celebrations which included flips and somersaults.

At sixteen he had sparred with Mark Epton, a Mexborough flyweight who after six wins out of six, was preparing for a British and European challenge. After two sessions with the youngster, the second one for real, Epton felt so demoralised, he opted out of boxing.

Spurning a chance to be in the 1992 Great Britain Olympic team, Naz was only interested in becoming a professional boxer as soon as he was old enough at eighteen. As a publicity stunt, the professional forms were signed in the House of Commons. Tony Blair being one of the MPs there to witness Hamed sign up a short fight deal with Barry Hearn. As far as he was concerned, this is where his career began and for a long time he had been counting the days until it happened. From the beginning, all the Prince Naseem trademarks that he would make his own were part of his media build up, right from the spectacular entrance, the vault over the ropes into the ring, the leopard skin trunks and the celebration dance at the end of the fight. Earning £1,000 for his first fight, his debut came at Mansfield in April 1992 against experienced professional, Ricky Beard from Dagenham. His manager Ingle was in the corner for the first time for, being in the professional game, he was barred from close to ring contact in Naz's fights as an amateur. Beard had never seen an opponent like him and in his fifteen years in the game had never been hit so hard. Beard lasted only two rounds and by the end of Naseem's first year in the paid ranks, five more opponents had been soundly beaten.

His sixth opponent, Peter Buckley, was the first man to stay the six round distance.

After only three fights, Naseem had made the European ratings and his six fights had all been planned in different boxing cities such as London, Manchester, Birmingham, Liverpool and Sunderland, so the news could carry far and wide about this devastating young boxer who was also soon attracting big revenue from the advertising world.

He raced to ten straight wins. Peter Buckley, the only boxer to go the distance with Naseem, was stopped in four rounds in Cardiff in the return bout. National sponsors were queuing up to be involved and already he had ended his association with Barry Hearn to sign up with Mickey Duff and later Frank Warren. Television was also becoming aware of his potential, for in his eleventh appearance he topped the bill, stopping Belgian John Miceli in two rounds in an ITV network broadcast fight.

It was appropriate that his first home town appearance was a championship fight for Naz had been matched as a challenger to European bantam champion Vincenzo Belcastro of Italy. One or two press pundits had speculated whether Naz could go twelve rounds and if there were any frailties, the Italian was definitely the man to expose them. Belcastro was a tough little bantam who had beaten the British champion, Drew Docherty, on his home ground in Glasgow. He'd been ranked sixth in the world and had taken part in fourteen title fights, including two unsuccessful world title fights and had never been knocked down. The champion was completely outboxed and made to look like a novice. Belcastro couldn't land a punch on him and the Italian went down three times during the course of the twelve rounds. The result of the fight was never in doubt and every round was credited to the challenger. What took away the edge of a great win was Naz's over-the-top showboating and mickey taking of the defeated champion.

Naz fought again in Sheffield three months later in his first European title defence when he easily beat Antonio Picard, the number one challenger. As predicted by the Prince who had stated in a Cassius Clay style pre-fight prediction, the round in which the fight would finish, the fight ended in the third, but not before the challenger had been down four times.

The title was never defended again, as Naz had decided to campaign in the super bantam division (8 stone 10lb).

In his first fight as a super bantam, for the vacant WBC international title, he took on a tough customer, Freddie Cruz of the Dominican Republic. Cruz was another fighter who had never been stopped and he did the wrong thing when he called the Sheffield boxer a child at the weigh-in. There was no posing from Naz this time, it was straight down to business and Cruz was finished by the sixth round.

Following the Cruz win, Hamed was boasting that he would be world champion inside a year and, in pursuit of this claim, he had in his sights Welshman, Steve Robinson, who since he had won the WBO featherweight title, had defended it several times including a twelve round win over Cruz. With that kind of self belief it was hard to get anyone to argue against the chances of him achieving it. While Robinson was taking his title defences up to seven, Naz raced through a series of five quick defences of his WBC international title, none of which went past four rounds. Moving up to featherweight would be no problem for Naz, who often sparred with middleweights and above, typically with stablemate Johnny Nelson who often joined him in the sparring. In his international title defences, other venues like Cardiff (Robinson's backyard), Glasgow, where he received hero worship and Shepton Mallett, where 5000 fans went wild, were used to help spread the fame of the young and exciting star who was fast becoming the most popular fighter in the country. However, nothing could rival the hero-worship Naseem received when he visited his father's home country in the Yemen, where the Prince Naseem Hamed mania was bordering on the hysterical. Awards and honours were heaped on him including the country's highest civilian

'Naz', in action during the All Yorkshire World Title Fight against Paul Ingle.

decoration. The military had to protect him and when he did a sparring session 30,000 wanted to see him in action.

Naz was not concerned that his clash with Robinson was to take place in Cardiff and he deliberately belittled the world champion prior to the fight, using tactics his idol Mohammed Ali had used early in his career. He preferred spectators to be against him and in Cardiff he was not to be disappointed. There were 16,000 of them at the fight, all rooting for Robinson. It just made Naz even more determined. Robinson had held the title for two and a half years, being matched for the title when champion Ruben Palacia had been forced to withdraw after testing positive for HIV. Once again, Hamed was able to deal out the humiliation as he posed with his hands down by his side taunting Robinson to hit him. After the teasing and an exhibition of the Ali shuffle, Naz almost finished it in round five. Robinson managed to survive to round eight when the referee ended his nightmare.

Naseem had taken just twenty paid fights to win a world title, although he wasn't able totally to bask in the glory of yet another brilliant display, for he was in trouble with the British Boxing Board of Control, for his goading of the defeated champion. Hamed's argument was that his goading tactics were part of his plan, to break his opponent's concentration.

He returned to his fans in Glasgow for his first defence. There was pre-fight talk about his right hand, but any worries were dispelled with a dramatic first round knockout of Said Iawal, a Nigerian southpaw who only lasted thirty-five seconds! Iawal had gone down with the first punch and the fight was the eighth shortest world title match ever.

Three months later, the seemingly impossible happened. Naseem was sent to the canvas in his second world title defence at Newcastle. 23-year-old Puerto Rican, Daniel Alicea, a fighter with an excellent amateur record and unbeaten in his fifteen professional fights, floored Naseem in the opening round with a big right hand. The punch had been one of the Prince's own tricks, beating his man with the counter punch. The only other time the champion had been in that position before had been in training when heavyweight Adam Fogerty, who was twice his weight, managed to do it. Naz bounced up immediately to let his opponent know about it.

A wound-up and embarrassed Naseem, finished the job in his predicted second round and he also proved what some critics had doubted, he could take a punch. The knock-down proved Hamed was human and the champion was disappointed it had happened on his first network TV showing in America, on a Warren/Don King tie up.

Alicea wasn't the hand-picked opponent Iawal had been.

Naseem took his third title defence to Dublin to fight former IBF (1991 to 1993) and WBC (1995) champion, the rugged Mexican Manuel Medina. The fight was not vintage Hamed, but he still managed to put down his man three times and win the fight by the eleventh round. Before the fight, Naz had suffered from a heavy cold but had dismissed his management's views that he ought to postpone the fight for a week. Hamed started to tire as the fight passed the middle stages and although Medina had his moments, it was still the champion who found the power and put the tough little Mexican down in the eleventh round at which point his seconds retired him.

Naz was back to his best in destroying Argentine, Remigo Molina, in two rounds in Manchester and was able to take his first step in unifying the featherweight title in his quest to become the ultimate champion, when he faced the current IBF champion Tom 'Boom Boom' Johnson in February 1997 in London.

Johnson was considered his toughest test yet and Naseem trained as hard, if not harder than he had done for some time.

With only two defeats from forty-eight fights, a four year reign as champion which had included eleven defences, Johnson's record looked impressive and Ingle dismissed reports that he might be past his sell-by date. After a round of finding each other out, it looked as if Naz might end it in the predicted third, when his speed and stance switches were proving difficult for Johnson to accommodate. The IBF champion countered strongly and shook Hamed off balance with a knock-down, but this had no bearing on the final outcome of the fight, as Hamed proved the stronger and ended it with a right uppercut in the eighth. America was now starting to take notice of the Sheffield based champion, not least the big, in more ways than one, promoter Don King who had backed Johnson.

A 32-year-old Sunderland man, Billy Hardy, who had twice fought for the IBF bantam title was Naz's first home challenger. Currently European champion, Hardy had beaten Steve Robinson to become number one challenger. Some of Hardy's comments in the press didn't go down too well, nor the fact that he was training at a rival camp in the city under the supervision of Glyn Rhodes and Herol Graham, both ex-Ingle men. The fight only lasted ninety-three seconds. Hardy had his nose broken with the first punch and two counts later it was all over.

Attempts to unify the featherweight division had come to nothing because the rival organisations refused to work together and because the IBF wanted control of the opponents he fought. Naseem decided to relinquish their belt.

Argentine, Pastor Maurin, was to have been Naz's next opponent in July 1997 in London. Five days before the fight, Maurin had his eye cut in sparring with his fellow countryman, Juan Cabrera. The sparring partner took his place but couldn't cope with Hamed's brilliance and in two rounds, the mismatch was over.

Following the success of the film that had been made locally, Frank Warren hit on the idea of putting on Sheffield's own 'Full Monty' show. Ten title fights on the same night and the bill titled 'Judgement Day', featured Johnny Nelson, Ryan Rhodes, Chris Eubank versus Joe Calzaghe, Paul Ingle versus Jonjo Irwin and Naseem versus Puerto Rican, Jose Badillo. The champion hadn't fought in his home town for three years and the Badillo fight was to be his first defence in the steel city. Badillo was quality. His only defeat had come in his fight against Tom Johnson and, even then, he had knocked Johnson down before finally being defeated.

Encouraged by boxing in front of his home town supporters, Hamed gave one of his best displays. Much more cautious than usual, Naz's punching power saw Badillo finished by round seven, when the Puerto Rican's corner threw in the towel.

It had been a burning ambition long before he turned professional to fight in America and, after several earlier prospects had fallen through, Frank Warren announced Naz was fighting at the legendary Madison Square Garden, six days before Christmas 1997, against former WBC champion, Kevin Kelley. The pair had already met for Kelley, who had beaten some good men in the featherweight ranks, had been at ringside for the 'Full Monty' show and the pair had traded insults. Throughout their careers, Naz and his best mate Ryan Rhodes had supported each other's fights, but because the unbeaten Rhodes' world title challenge was only six days before in Sheffield, Naz, whose training camp was in the States, was the subject of a high media profile and couldn't accompany Brendan Ingle back home for Ryan's first world title fight.

Rhodes was able to make the trip back with Ingle, but it was a subdued Ryan because his unbeaten record was in tatters. Hamed couldn't live up to the hype, which had included an incredible 22ft high billboard portrait of him in Times Square and he upset purists in some quarters by claiming he had more skills than Mohammed Ali. The fight was unconvincing against one of his better opponents and after both fighters had been down three times, Naseem was still champion and unbeaten with a fourth round knock-out and as usual, the press made more of the knock-downs than his winning an exciting fight.

Another effort at unification came to nothing when 37-year-old Wilfrid Vazquez, another Puerto Rican, was stripped of his title by the WBA, before the fight, for not fighting the official WBA number one challenger. Once again Hamed's power was too much for the challenger and Vazquez went down four times by round seven at which point the referee had seen enough and stopped the fight.

For his second fight in 1998, and his eleventh defence of his WBO title, Naz had a second try at winning over the American fans. Again hype was to the fore and the Americans wanted to exploit the Halloween date of his Atlantic City clash with Belfast's former WBC bantam champion Wayne McCullough. Again he failed to grasp his chances in the world boxing headquarters. He beat McCullough, who was having his first fight as featherweight, on points by a large margin. However, the fight was one of the least impressive of all his fights. The unanimous decision was booed loudly by the big contingent of Irishmen in the 8,000 crowd. Before the fight Hamed had hurt his hand (the reason for the six month gap in between fights) which was the probable reason for his ring rustiness. Once again the American press were critical, although no one could argue with a record of thirty-one fights, thirty-one wins including twenty-eight knock-outs.

Yorkshireman, Paul Ingle, was given the next chance to fight Naz in Manchester and he did much better than Naz's other British opponent, Billy Hardy. Despite producing his sledgehammer finish in round eleven, Hamed was again criticised for his performance and there were reports that the 'Old Naz' would have seen off Ingle a lot earlier. Both Hamed's hands had swollen during the fight and from early on, he had suffered the discomfort of a cut inside his mouth. Ingle himself proved his worth by winning his own world title in 1999.

For some time there had been friction between Naz and his mentor, Brendan Ingle, and for a while Brendan had trained him. Now sadly their long association was over and Naseem was trained by American, Manny Steward. His new trainer had helped the careers of over thirty world champions. Steward stated that his new charge had the most powerful single punch in the business and could still be the legend he craved to be. Hamed spent six weeks in the Pennsylvania mountains under Steward for his next fight against theMexican WBA champion, Cesar Soto in Detroit. Sonto had never been knocked down. The action was widely reported as resembling a street brawl and Hamed teetered on the brink of disqualification. He lost points for persistently holding and even worse, he body slammed Soto in wrestling style. Naseem's points win had given him boxing's most prestigious title, while Soto who had lost his WBC title at his first defence claimed he was still champion and there should be a rematch.

The Soto fight was the Prince's last fight in the twentieth century. It looked as if he would have to give up his WBC title because his new controlling body wouldn't recognise the WBO to whom, after thirteen defences, Hamed felt a loyalty.

Early in the new year he announced that he would retire by 2002 and despite three unsuccessful attempts to win over the American fans, his main ambition was still to crack America, although any attempts to unify the featherweight division seemed very remote.

Whatever happens for Prince Naseem Hamed in the new century, he leaves the old one as certainly the most colourful character yet in British boxing and with few equals as one of the most devastating punchers of all time.

JONJO IRWIN

Over the years, there have been some classy featherweights to come out of Yorkshire and in the later years of the 1990s, the white rose county could boast some of the best. Prince Naseem had completed an unbeaten run to the world title. Naz's rival Paul Ingle followed on with a second title, and making a great trio, John, who boxed as Jonjo Irwin, the Denaby born, Doncaster based battler who after climaxing an outstanding amateur career with gold at the Auckland Commonwealth Games, went on to become Doncaster's first British champion since the immediate postwar days of Bruce Woodcock, half a century earlier. He was later to emulate Johnny Cuthbert's 1920s feat of winning the British featherweight title twice.

It was always hoped by the acknowledged experts of the boxing fraternity that Jonjo Irwin would take the professional path. Irwin had expected to round off his glittering amateur career by boxing in the Barcelona Olympics, but when he was controversially left out of the Great Britain team, after failing to qualify for the world championships in Sydney, the South Yorkshire council worker became a professional sooner than he had visualised. Jonjo, who captained his country sixteen times in international contests, boxed out of the Tom Hill Amateur Club and had started under trainer, Ernie Oxer's guidance when aged only eight. Ernie was a man who had put in fifty years' service to boxing in Denaby and there could have been no one prouder than the old coach, when John went up to collect his Commonwealth medal in New Zealand. There was a rumpus at the ceremony when Australian, James Nicolson, stepped into the winner's place in protest against his disqualification. For two pins Jonjo was in the mood to teach the cocky Aussie a lesson there and then.

Irwin joined the paid ranks under local managers, John Rushton and Pete Thompson and made his debut on a Christine Rushton promotion. His opponent was supposed to be Welshman, Miguel Matthews, but he failed to show at the Doncaster Dome fight.

Kid McAuley, who like Irwin had just become a professional and had turned up to watch, was persuaded to return home for his kit. Jonjo's fight was duly put down the bill and he beat his Liverpool born

Jonjo Irwin, who twice won the British featherweight title.

stablemate, who had done most of his boxing in the RAF in six round matches. Matthews did turn up three weeks later and Irwin scored his second points win. When he stopped his third opponent, Colin Lynch, in his second Doncaster appearance, Lynch's manager, Paddy Byrne, was forecasting Irwin would be champion within two years.

Two inside the distance wins, including one against the heavier Alfreton fighter G.G. Goddard, saw Barry Hearn, head of the Matchroom organisation, become John's joint manager. After another victory over Kid McAuley, the second meeting being for the vacant All Ireland featherweight title, John suffered his first defeat at the Midlands Sporting Club, in Solihull. Ahead on points, Irwin received a badly cut eye after a head clash in the sixth round in a top of the bill bout with Kevin Middleton, who had recovered from a first round knock down.

Returning to Solihull for a win over Pete Buckley, Jonjo then made his first London appearance against a four pounds heavier Peter Harris, the former featherweight champion of the late 1980s. It was a close affair and Irwin took the verdict by just half a point. He suffered a second setback when Derek Amory beat him in two rounds in Belfast, but his recent progress earned him a crack at a new title, the WBO Penta Continental super featherweight title.

John was to have met Glasgow fighter Wilson Docherty, who had won the vacant title beating Paul Harvey and had defended it against Peter Harris at the Dome. When Docherty cried off with flu, Michael Armstrong came in to fight Jonjo for the vacant title. The hard punching Armstrong was no pushover and Irwin did well to contain him but he did, steadily building up what became a points win. When he beat the much more experienced Harry Escott in his first defence in London, manager Rushton stated that his man had never boxed better, Rushton's man controlled the fight from beginning to end in his second defence, recording a points win over Dagenham based African, Banama Dibateza.

Fighting twelve rounders had become a regular event as Jonjo won another title going the distance for the fourth fight running. Again, Wilson Docherty should have been his opponent, but after he pulled out with a shoulder injury and after a fight with Laurenao Riminez (from the Dominican Republic, record twenty wins out of twenty-two fights, one loss to Naseem Hamed), failed to materialise, Madrid based Manuel Calvo, who had won twelve out of thirteen fights to Irwin's eleven out of thirteen, was the Doncaster based man's new opponent for the WBO inter continental featherweight title. Calvo was a creditable opponent, who made it difficult for the local man, though John's winning margin was larger than expected. There was a quick defence of his new title, for seventeen days later he defeated Trinidad's Learie Bruce in eight, one sided rounds.

Whereas other boxers used Inter-Continental titles to go on to higher things, Jonjo had an ambition to become a British champion and his unbeaten run of title wins saw him matched with featherweight champion, Michael Deveney, who was defending the title after winning it from Wilson Docherty at Potters Bar. The same week Chris Saunders had brought a British title to the area. Jonjo emulated him making the referee's decision easy by winning eleven rounds out of twelve. It was a brave effort because the Denaby man had damaged his hand early in the fight and had managed to keep it quiet.

After Doncaster had given him a civic reception, Jonjo got down to serious preparation for the first defence of his new title, which was expected to be against Elvis Parsley or former WBO champion, Colin McMillan.

Midland based Parsley got the opportunity to be Irwin's first challenger and the 33-year-old Walsall man in the twilight of his career, met Jonjo in London. Parsley proved too limited an opponent as the Doncaster man contained the fight throughout. The bout terminated when Parsley, whom Irwin made miss more times that he hit, was finished in round eight. Colin McMillan was another 30-year-old challenger for Jonjo's chance to win the Lonsdale Belt outright, although he was a step above Elvis Parsley. McMillan was on the comeback trail after being out for thirteen months with a shoulder dislocation. The pair met at Goresbrook Leisure Centre. Although McMillan looked pale from the form that had made him world champion in 1992, there were flashes from boxing's once golden boy. McMillan, who collapsed afterwards, had to dig deep and Jonjo thought he had won. McMillan won the points decision and the British title by only half a point.

Disappointed at losing his domestic title in such a close decision, Jonjo had the chance to win yet another title in his next appearance when he fought for the vacant Commonwealth title. Nothing was known of his West African opponent Smith Adoom, whose London debut was his first fight outside Africa. McMillan turned up at the ringside with a claim that he was champion and should be in the ring with Adoom. Jonjo answered him by throwing down the gauntlet for a return. After yet another twelve round points win, Irwin wanted to make his first defence in front of his own fans at the Dome. He was supposed to have met Canadian, Barrington Francis, but instead met Australian Rick Rayner, who had fought for the title before losing an eight round decision to Billy Hardy in 1992, the only time the Australian had ever been stopped. The local man entertained his fans at the Dome in style and the fight was regarded as one of the best domestic scraps of the year. A points victory was the seventh time Jonjo had gone twelve rounds to achieve a title win in a successful defence.

Three weeks after the Rayner fight, McMillan lost his title to another Yorkshireman, the unbeaten Paul Ingle from Scarborough.

An all white rose clash with Ingle was a natural and by the time they met in Sheffield in October 1997, Ingle was going for an outright Lonsdale Belt, having beaten Michael Aldis in his first defence. Both men put their titles up for grabs (Irwin didn't put up his Inter-Continental title for Rushton had criticised the organisers who wanted him to defend against Ceasar Guemax, a Mexican, for 'peanuts' and it was decided to relinquish the title rather than comply). The fight was on one of Frank Warren's extravaganza's at Sheffield and because the running order of the fights was changed, the fight at one time looked as if it wouldn't take place. Warren's licence had run out at 1.00am and the two fighters had to wait twenty minutes whilst Warren sorted out matters with the police to allow the fight to proceed. It had been scheduled for 9.00pm, but was changed to suit TV commitments with Mexico. Irwin ran out of steam and was forced to retire against the unbeaten Scarborough man in round eight, tiring visibly as the fight started to reach the later stages.

The self-employed joiner and his mentor Rushton started a campaign for a return, when it was learned that Ingle had failed a dope test after the fight. Fining him £2,000, the British Boxing Board of Control accepted his explanation that he had taken the drug, frusemide, as treatment for a swollen ankle. Rushton was furious. He campaigned with his MP with the reasoning that the £2,000, fine said he was guilty and the fight result should be annulled. The British Boxing Board of Control, ordered a rematch, but Ingle wanted to relinquish, for there were bigger pay packets and titles to seek against the likes of Naseem Hamed and Billy Hardy.

Irwin also wanted a piece of the same action and challenges were issued to the same fighters. It was Jonjo's dream to meet Naz. Whilst Ingle defended his Commonwealth crown and with his future being a world title fight with Hamed and later his own world title, Jonjo was matched for the vacant British title with another Yorkshire based fighter.

Esham Pickering was the latest Brendan Ingle/Frank Warren protégé and had earned his right to a title fight with a win over Michael Deveney in Glasgow. Young Pickering was trying to emulate a record, for a decade earlier Paul Hodgkinson had won a British title after only twelve fights. The Newark born Pickering had won his first eleven. When Ryan Rhodes pulled out of the Sheffield date, Jonjo and Pickering were elevated to top of the bill. Ten days before the fight, Irwin damaged his left hand in sparring and was only able to shadow box up to the fight. Pained throughout the fight, he still managed to throw more punches than Pickering. Jonjo won his Lonsdale Belt and though Pickering had been second best in his points defeat, he would learn and come again.

Steve Robinson, who had looked invincible in his two and a half years as a WBO featherweight champion, until he stepped into the ring against Naseem, was still a big name in the featherweight ranks. Rushton was pleased when the British Boxing Board of Control sanctioned a meeting with the Welshman, but upset when Robinson decided that the first thing on his agenda was a rematch with Hamed or a fight with Ingle, who had recently beaten the other main featherweight, Billy Hardy.

In fact, it was Ingle who got the big fight with Hamed and while Rushton was obviously upset that his man, who in his opinion at 29 was boxing better than he was at twenty-one, had been overlooked, there was another British title defence to be made.

Again he was matched with another inexperienced challenger in Liverpool's Alex Moon, who had only had fourteen fights as a professional. As expected Jonjo had too much class for him and looked far more convincing than the 117-114 winning margin. Moon's plan had been to catch Irwin early, but the shrewd Denaby man was well aware of his tactics and denied him the opportunity.

Whilst Jonjo was keen to move up to European level and possibly relinquish his British title, the idea was floated again of a clash with Steve Robinson. The Welshman had never won a British title, a situation which at one time would have been unheard of, for originally you had to prove your claim for world honours by winning at least British titles and, more times than not, European titles as well before being able to challenge for a world title fight.

John dearly wanted the fight to take place at the Dome, but failure to agree on terms with Barry Hearn, delayed matters and eventually Manchester got the fight. A fight with Junior Jones for a version of the world title was turned down because Robinson was rated number two WBO challenger and a win over a boxer of his stature could see Jonjo leap-frog him and be first in line for a lucrative crack with Naseem, whom Rushton freely talked of his own man beating.

Over 400 fans made the journey from Doncaster across the Pennines to cheer on the Conisborough based boxer and whilst Robinson bragged of knocking Jonjo out, Rushton was confident Jonjo's jab would lead him to victory. In reality he left himself too much to do in the latter stages of the fight. Lacking the quality of his earlier fights, he showed Robinson too much respect and paid the penalty. Robinson's know-how in the late rounds saw him gain a points victory and leave Jonjo Irwin's world title hopes at least for 1999 on the shelf.

CLINTON WOODS

The year 1999 threw up two major shocks in the British boxing scene that affected South Yorkshire. There was Ryan Rhodes' second round defeat at the hands of the 'Method Man' Jason Matthews, and a rise from local fame to national level for Clinton Woods, who won British, European and British Commonwealth titles at one bite in only his third fight at light heavyweight, after the 6ft 2in Mexborough fighter had started his career in the super middleweight ranks.

Boxing since the age of seven and a Yorkshire schools' champion at twelve, young Clinton was deprived of an opponent for twelve months at thirteen years of age, because no kid would get in the ring with him. Ray Gillat, his trainer at the Hillsborough Boys' Club, even advertised, but still no one wanted to know. Gillat kept him busy sparring with sixteen and seventeen-year-olds and running four miles every night. When he did return to the ring again after a year, he won a regional title. Always carrying an ambition to be a professional boxer, he signed as a professional for manager and promoter Dennis Hobson, with Neil Part becoming his trainer.

He quickly became a popular, and almost cult figure, at the boxing promotions at the Pinegrove Club where, after his early performances, he became a bill topper and full house guarantor.

A twelve match unbeaten start with half the wins coming inside the distance, saw Clinton fight for the vacant Central Area title against Bradford's Craig Joseph at the Pinegrove. The Bradford social worker, and a late starter in the boxing world at twenty-eight, gave a good account of himself and Clint had to pull out all the stops in the hard fought action to take the title. Not long after, Joseph decided the boxing scene wasn't for him and he joined a 'Drifters type' cabaret group. The Pinegrove was a sell-out when Woods met Darren Littlewood for his Central Area defence. Darren was from the rival gym in Wincobank and Brendan Ingle's man who hailed from the Parson Cross BBC and had won half of his twelve contests. Clint beat him on a stoppage in round six and, with a fifteen match undefeated run, the Sheffield man was nearing a title fight. The Pinegrove was the scene for his next fight and Dave Ashton did well

Clinton Woods, with the British Commonwealth and European Light Heavyweight belts title.

to last the distance after Woods' explosive left hook had put him down in the first minute. An easier than expected win against Danny Juma, the Belfast based African and a points win over Jeff Finlayson, saw Clinton get the break he was after.

Former ABA holder Dave Starie was due to fight Sidcup's Mark Baker, for the vacant Commonwealth super middleweight title. Starie withdrew and Clinton took the fight on the Herol Graham versus Vinnie Pazienza card at Wembley, and celebrated his first appearance in the capital by bringing home the Commonwealth title to Sheffield, a title that Henry Wharton had held from 1991 to 1997.

Four months after his Wembley win, Clinton met David Starie at Hull in his first defence of his new title. The 23-year-old Suffolk ringman had a year previously been considered the country's glittering prospect until Dean Francis had taken his British super middleweight title off him. Starie was on the comeback trail and with a record showing fifteen wins from sixteen bouts, he was still a top drawer challenger. In the same weekend local fans were saddened to hear that 'Bomber' Graham had failed to win a world title in his comeback attempt, his third unsuccessful try.

Starie took away Woods's Commonwealth title and unbeaten record. Composed throughout, Starie never tired, even when Clinton made a late surge. The winning margin was 117 points to 113. Explaining his man's lack-lustre performance, Dennis Hobson, confirming that his man had made hard work of it and that he had done well to go the distance said 'It just wasn't Clinton's night. He looked tailor made for Starie's style'.

It had been thought for a while that Clinton's 6ft 2in frame would be more suited to the light heavyweight division, so three months on from his Commonwealth defeat, Woods made his home town debut as a light heavyweight against Pete Mason of Hartlepool. Weighing 12 stone 7lb, and looking sharp at his new weight, Clinton retired Mason at the end of the fourth round. Thirty-four-year-old Leeds boxer, Crawford Ashley (sometimes referred to as Ashley Crawford), who had been a professional since 1987 and in his time fought twice for world titles, had reclaimed his British light heavyweight title and more recently obtained Commonwealth and European crown's, was the obvious target for manager Hobson. Ashley refused for, with the news that Henry Wharton was moving up the division, a tussle with Henry would be a more lucrative attraction, especially in Leeds.

The best way to challenge Ashley was to become the number one contender with the Boxing Board and for his second fight in his new division, Clinton was awarded an official eliminator with Mark Smallwood of Atherstone at Bowlers nightclub in Manchester. The self-managed Smallwood was undefeated in fifteen bouts and the fight with Woods was his biggest test yet.

Clinton's non-stop tactics, when he gained the advantage in round five saw the Midlands' man worn down and the fight was stopped in round seven.

Henry Wharton's subsequent retirement saw Clint's fight with Crawford Ashley become a definite starter and after a Crawford viral illness delayed the fight for a month, Clinton met the man with the record of thirty-one wins out of forty, including twenty-seven knock-outs and who still dreamed of ending his career with a third tilt at a world title. Clinton was to shatter those dreams when he stopped the old campaigner, sending him on the road to retirement. Woods' chin withstanding everything that Ashley could throw at it. Suffering a cut early on, Woods bravely fought himself back into the fight which ended in round eight, when Crawford's corner saved him from further punishment by throwing in the towel, leaving Clinton in his 23rd fight, a triple champion.

The stamina criticism aimed at him after the Starie fight was answered with much of the credit going to the training sessions with Howard Rainey at Attercliffe and Don Valley boxing centre.

Clinton ended 1999 with two defences of the Commonwealth title. He topped the bill for the first time in London and beat New Zealander, Sam Leuli, in six rounds, then in a Sheffield appearance he met the devout Christian, John Lennox Lewis, from Trinidad whom he also stopped.

Clinton ended 1999 with the following World rankings, the third in the WBC, fifth in the the WBA and sixth in the WBO and with every prospect of a world title fight in 2000.

RYAN RHODES

WHILE PRINCE NASEEM HAMED was making his meteoric rise to world stardom, following fast in his Sheffield footsteps came Naz's close friend and boyhood pal from the pair's very early days in Brendan Ingle's Wincobank gym. Ryan Rhodes, a professional as soon as he was old enough to be one, a fearsome puncher, whose fights seldom last the distance, very quickly reached the top of the British boxing tree.

A couple of defeats have tested his staying power in the world ranks, but with one of the best men in the business in Brendan Ingle in his corner and youth on his side, it would be no surprise to see Ryan Rhodes return and earn an extended run on the world's stage.

Two and a half years younger than Naz, Ryan was only six when he started to attend Brendan's Saturday morning classes. Like Frank Bruno, young Rhodes always claimed his interest in boxing had saved him from a possible 'naughty boy' life, for several of his old schoolmates ended up in prison. Like Naz (Brendan never liked them sparring together), young Ryan was taken all over whilst still a schoolboy and he was in Spain and heartbroken, when his idol Herol Graham lost to Julian Jackson in a world title fight. Ryan boxed out of the Unity Boys' Club and was untouchable as a schoolboy the titles reeled off. NBC, school national, junior national and four national amateur titles were part of a formidable teenage record and he became a hero for a different reason, for whilst on holiday on a Greek Island, he rescued a woman who had been swept out to sea. So impressed were the England team management with Ryan, that they elected him to become captain of the England team to fight in Russia.

The lads at *The Crown Inn* on Penistone Road, were behind young Ryan and raised £400 to enable him to make the trip.

It had been decided very early on that Ryan would become a professional and the young Sheffielder couldn't wait until he was eighteen.

Ryan made his paid debut in Wales against Lee Crocker, who had a fierce reputation as a puncher. The youngster had the Cardiff fans on the edge of their seats as Crocker went down twice in round one and was stopped in the following round.

It was no surprise when in one round, middleweight Shamus Casey went in Ryan's next fight, for the all action Casey had won only two of his last thirty-four fights (in the middle of 1998, Casey's fourteen year record read 160 fights, won 29, drawn 5 and 126 defeats). There was criticism that young Rhodes was deliberately being fed fighters with poor form to build up his unbeaten record.

Roy Chipperfield had only won one of his nine professional fights when he lasted only a round and Martin Jolley, whom Ryan beat twice in quick sucession in his seventh and eighth fights, was another boxer with a similar record.

Though he was getting to the back end of his career, Del Bryan, welterweight champion twice, had a much better pedigree. Ingle had plotted his downfall the year previously when his man, Chris Saunders, took away his welterweight title. Rhodes beat Bryan on points

Ryan Rhodes the Sheffield youngster with a brilliant schoolboy record. *(Photo loaned by Bill Matthews).*

and there was talk of future TV exposure, for Frank Warren had kept an interested eye on the Sheffield middleweight's unbeaten start.

In his eleventh fight, and not yet two years into his professional career, Ryan was given the chance to become British champion only a month after his twentieth birthday.

The big talking point for the Sheffield fight fans was, would Paul 'Silky' Jones, himself a Sheffield lad, have too much experience for the youngster. For Jones, who was exactly ten years and a day older, had been the WBO light middleweight champion only a year earlier and hadn't actually lost his title in the ring.

The all Sheffield pairing was for the British light middleweight title.

Glyn Rhodes, who ran the Hillsborough based Sheffield boxing centre and a man who once refused to train Herol Graham, was in 'Silky's' corner for the Ponds Forge encounter. Paul had to shed some ounces before the fight, though it didn't seem to affect him as the match was fairly even, until it reached the eighth round. Ryan knew a lot of 'Silky's' moves, for he had been in the ring sparring with Jones when he was a teenager. A straight left floored the former world champion as Rhodes switched from southpaw to orthodox. Two big rights forced the referee to intervene and a delighted Frank Warren was forecasting a "Naz" type rise for the new title holder, who was the youngest British champion for fifty-seven years.

Ryan Rhodes made a statement saying he wanted to win a Lonsdale Belt outright inside ninety days, quicker than anyone else had. His aim was to beat the current holder of the fastest time, lightweight champion Michael Ayers. Another Yorkshireman. Central Area light middleweight champion, Peter Waudby had won his eliminator to fight Rhodes in front of his own Hull supporters and there was a big following from the east coast to witness their man's challenge. Ryan sent them home very disappointed as he confirmed his top of the bill rating when he blasted the Hull fireman, who entered the ring on the back of five wins and was obviously up for a fight, in one round. Del Bryan, whom Ryan had beaten on points in his fight before the title win, was named as his second challenger. The first fight had been close, with only half a point in it, but this time Rhodes' punches sent Bryan a step nearer to retirement when he finished it in round seven, Bryan's fifth successive defeat. Confirming the record belt time, Ryan was full of praise for the old champion who gave him a hard battle for nearly two thirds of the fight.

There was a new title for Ryan Rhodes the following month, though there was some difficulty in finding him an opponent for his IBF inter-continental challenge. Ilford boxer, Nicky Thurbin, unbeaten in his first fifteen fights, withdrew with a cut eye and first substitute, American Kevin Lowther also pulled out. The thirty-year-old Lindon Scarlett got the match. Scarlett wasn't in the same class and Rhodes' fourteenth successive win, his third which had failed to go beyond round one and his tenth inside the distance, was a formality.

In a quest for world honours, Ryan dropped his British light middleweight title and Manchester's Ensley Bingham, who had done exactly the same thing a year before, returned to win the title a second time. Bingham had lost on points in his home town challenge for Ronald Wright's WBO light middleweight title and there was speculation that Bingham, another fighter nearing his mid thirties, would meet Ryan in a 'war of the roses' official world eliminator.

Ryan dedicated his second IBF inter-continental win to his favourite uncle, Dennis, who had recently died.

American, Ed Griffin who was listed as a welterweight, also felt the

Yorkshireman's punching power, when he couldn't survive past two rounds at Barnsley's Metrodome. Deciding to operate in the more attractive full middleweight ranks, yet another Rhodes fight failed to last past round two when Ryan took out Russian, Yuri Epifantsev, in a WBO middleweight eliminator. Ryan's right hand put the Russian champion in trouble in the opening round, with the referee deciding he had seen enough in the second calling a halt to the proceedings. Rhodes' quick win didn't meet the approval of all the Sheffield faithful. Proving that you can't please everybody in a 12,000 crowd, a minority demonstrated their fickleness over a short contest, though the majority showed approval of Ryan's explosive and quality finishing.

Rhodes didn't get his fight with the WBO champ, Lonnie Bradley, for the American was stripped because of his unavailability due to a detached retina. Ryan was matched with Otis Grant, the Jamaican born, Montreal based Canadian, who rejoiced under the nickname 'Magic'. Interest was enough in the booming boxing city for Frank Warren to put the fight on at the 18,000 capacity Ponds Forge. Grant had only lost one out of thirty-one bouts and he had beaten some good ringmen and was easily Ryan's toughest opponent to date. The big disappointment to Ryan was that his big mate 'Naz' couldn't be at ringside. The pair had always supported each other, but Hamed was in America, preparing for his stateside debut at the legendary Madison Square Garden a few days later.

Brendan Ingle was a busy man, he had been in America, putting 'Naz' through his paces in preparation for his much publicised debut, before returning to Sheffield for Ryan's fight and then straight back to the States for Prince's fight with Kevin Kelley.

Grant was another boxer over thirty and this time experience did tell. Rhodes came strong in the later stages but for once his powerful punching couldn't finish his man. Ryan had been 'old man'd' by a good professional and it was an expensive lesson, for an unbeaten record and a world title had been lost. There was a little bit of consolation for Ryan. He was able to fly out to America and cheer on his mate to his first stateside victory.

After six months out of the ring Ryan, keen to re-establish himself in the world rankings, returned on the Chris Eubank versus Carl Thompson bill to meet the Hungarian holder of the WBO inter-continental title, Lorent Szabo. Ryan had witnessed Szabo end Jason Matthew's three fight winning sequence as champion four months earlier, when Szabo took everything Matthews could throw at him before responding by knocking Matthews out. Ryan predicted he would beat Szabo in four rounds. Though he didn't do that, he stopped him a few rounds later. It was good to return to winning ways.

The 27-year-old Mexican, Fidel Avendeno, who was a substitute for American, Manuel Esparza, was expected to be a tough test and possibly take Ryan the distance in Rhodes' defence of his new title. A professional since he was seventeen, the Mexican had won forty-six out of fifty-seven fights and had taken Olympic boxer David Reid the distance. Rhodes had been sparring with the two stone heavier John Keeton and the benefit seemed to show when the Sheffield man's copybook right hand was followed by a killer left hook presenting the Hillsborough crowd with yet another early finish.

With Sheffield boasting two world champions in 1999 in Naseem Hamed and Johnny Nelson, Ryan's explosive punching had put him in the frame to be the city's third. The only blot on his record, Otis Grant, had been stripped for moving up a weight and after it had been mooted that they should meet in an eliminator, Ryan was matched with the unbeaten German, Bert Schenk, who was rated seventh in the WBC ratings for the vacant title. The Doncaster Dome was proud to announce their first world title fight and a confident Ryan moved out to Grand Canaria to concentrate on his training, little knowing that a late withdrawal and substitution would leave his world title dream in tatters. Schenk developed a back injury and British fighter, Jason Matthews took his place at less than a week's notice.

It was obvious something had to give for the two big punchers had won thirty-seven out of forty-one wins in knockouts between them. Like Ryan, who was odds on favourite, Matthews had only lost once. Matthews wasn't going to waste his opportunity and in one of the boxing upsets of the year, Ryan was flattened in two rounds, the first time he had ever been stopped. The shock result was felt in the crowd and there were several hospital cases as fighting broke out among Ryan's angered followers. It was known Ryan had suffered a series of personal problems including the suicide of his uncle and though in no way was it offered as an excuse, it was believed by those close to him that Ryan's mind wasn't fully on the job in hand.

Provided he can come back from the Jason Matthews setback, and at still only twenty-three, Ryan's punching power alone should ensure that he has a big part to play in the top circle of boxing in the new century.